# THE AGEING DOG

Helping your Dog through the Golden Years

CARL GORMAN BVSc MRCVS

HENSTON

First published 1995
© Henston Ltd, 1995

ISBN 1 85054 098 5

Henston Ltd, The Chequers, 2 Church Street, High Wycombe, Bucks, England

Printed and bound by Henry Ling Limited, Dorchester, England

Cover design by CBA & Associates

Cover illustration by Bob Cox

Dog sketches by Andrea Schrader

# Contents

# List of figures

> **Key:**
> ➡ **Heavy type and arrows indicate sign/symptom**
> ⟵ Lighter type and arrows indicate disease/condition

# List of tables

# Foreword

The significance of the outward signs of ageing in our canine companion often escapes our immediate attention. Increasing breathlessness during exercise, for example, or deteriorating dental condition, is usually insidious and only begins to give us cause for concern when body systems start to fail and clinical problems arise. By then it is often too late to do much about it and the inexorable decline starts to gather pace.

With a little thought and foresight, often starting as early as eight years of age, the quality of these later years can be enhanced. Anticipation of the problems and alterations in management and lifestyle as well as prompt veterinary attention can ensure that instead of your dog becoming a burden to himself, he can continue to enjoy a quality of life he deserves after the years of pleasure and companionship he has given.

Carl Gorman's special interest in these important years of our dogs' lives has allowed him to prepare this comprehensive text covering all aspects of the care of the ageing dog. His easy to understand style of presentation and the content makes this title essential reading for all caring dog owners as their dog's years advance.

Allan J Henderson BVM&S MRCVS
Editor, Henston Ltd

# Acknowledgement

The editorial team of Henston would like to thank C-Vet Veterinary Products for their support without which this publication could not have been produced.

C-Vet Veterinary Products, suppliers of:

| | | |
|---|---|---|
| Citadel dog vaccines | Zenecarp Injection | Zenecarp Tablets |
| Corventa-D | Diuride | Sectine |
| Hylashine | OxyDex | Tarlite |
| Kerect | DermPlus | PLT |

and many other products, to the veterinary surgeon.

All brand names are trade marks of the Company.

# Introduction

Advice is readily available from any number of sources for owners of new puppies. We are usually keen to accept or consider this advice to ensure that we start our dog off in life in the best possible manner. Puppyhood, however, lasts only for 12-18 months, after which your dog becomes an adult and should be able to look after himself. Old age, on the other hand, may last for half of our dog's life, or even more.

As dogs enter old age and begin to feel its effects, they are often treated in the same way as they always have been, with love and with their basic needs provided for, but without regard for their changing requirements. Older dogs work differently as changes in metabolism occur, but if we attend to the developing problems as they arise, we can help them to feel youthful for longer, and as fit and comfortable as possible throughout their later years.

One of the saddest things I hear is to be told that an older dog's symptoms are 'just old age', meaning that they are to be expected and therefore just accepted. Our canine friends are the most long suffering and uncomplaining of companions, who will seldom cry to us that they suffer from the agonies of arthritis, the pain and fever of bad teeth and infected gums, or the nausea and discomfort of kidney failure. It is for us to notice their symptoms, and our responsibility to do all we can to relieve them.

In this book I would like to explain the processes by which our dogs age, and what it means to them. By knowing what to expect and what steps we can take to keep elderly dogs in the best of health, we can reward our most faithful friends with as comfortable and fulfilling an old age as possible.

## Author's thanks

I would like to thank the people whose inspiration, help and encouragement has enabled me to write this book. Allan Henderson for sympathetic and sensible editing. The publishing team at Henston for turning a manuscript into a book. My wife, Suzanne, for help with organisation and ideas.

I am grateful to my clients and patients who have taught me what people would like to know about the care of an aged dog. Also, my own two dogs, whose recent qualification as geriatrics, has sharpened my interest in the subject even further.

I would also like to express my thanks to C-Vet for their support without which this publication could not have been produced.

Carl Gorman BVSc MRCVS

# CHAPTER 1 Recognising the ageing dog

## What is ageing?

Taken most simply, ageing merely means 'getting old'. But why should getting old matter to a dog? Why should it be worse for a dog of 10 to become 2 years older rather than for a 2 year old to gain those same two years? The answer is that ageing is at one and the same time both a natural process and the result of an accumulation of disease processes and natural wastage which result in the less efficient operation of the body. By the time a dog is in its later years, reduction in the efficiency of its body will have reached the point where it can no longer disguise it, and signs of failing limbs or organs may become noticeable.

This means that many of the changes in your dog which you may notice as it grows older can't just be passed off as 'getting old'. There is a reason for each and every symptom of ageing and while we may not be able to relieve all of them, there are many that we can do something for.

The purpose of this book is to explain those reasons and give some practical advice on what can be done to make your best friend's old age more comfortable for him and rewarding for both of you.

## Why does a dog age?

As our dog grows older its body will undergo various irreversible changes to its structure and function. This comes about for several reasons.

a) The number of functioning cells in each organ will gradually decline. As older cells in organs become worn out and die, not all will be replaced. Indeed once some organs have reached their mature size, their cells will never be replaced; for instance nervous tissue (including the brain) and the kidneys.

1

b)   As well as there being fewer functioning cells, the cells which make up each organ will slowly become less efficient. One reason is that they contain fewer enzymes which enable them to carry out their functions. Another is that they themselves become less efficient through the deterioration of the physical microstructures that make up each cell.

c)   Cell mutations (changes in structure) occur naturally about once every million cell divisions. As a body gets older it accumulates more of these mutant cells, which will themselves divide to form clusters of abnormal cells. Most of these cells do not function in the way they were meant to, and so reduce the efficiency of the organ containing them. Some of these mutant cells are, however, the start of cancer and will grow to form tumours.

d)   The body and its organs suffer much injury during a lifetime. This can be either physical trauma such as with joint injuries or as a result of infection which leaves scarred, non-functional areas of tissue. Kidney infections earlier in life, for example, may not be severe enough to cause actual disease, yet may kill many irreplaceable kidney cells.

As old age proceeds, more of the above changes will have taken place, and more signs of old age will be apparent.

# Rates of ageing

Individual animals age at different rates. Some have a better genetic make up than others so that, for instance, one which inherits a tendency to bad hip conformation (hip dysplasia) will probably suffer arthritis of these joints before another which had perfect hips to start with. Environmental influences will also have some bearing on the rate of decline of body function. A dog which is well cared for, well fed and well protected against diseases is likely to be stronger and healthier so increasing its chances of living longer than a less fortunate animal.

# When does old age start?

As with people there is great variation between the chronological ages of different dogs and their physical state. As a rule the giant breeds have a relatively short life span, whilst some small Terriers and Toy Poodles may reach 20. As we have already discussed however, individuals of the same breed may have quite different life expectancies depending on their breeding and their care during their younger years. It is useful, however, to have an age at which one can start to think of your dog as starting to get old and so begin to prepare for its golden years.

The average life expectancy of dogs is now a little above 13 years of age. Dogs are generally thought of as entering old age when they are about 8. This is the age when their organs are beginning to feel the effect of the ageing processes described. This may or may not be obvious to us yet, as many organs have great excess capacity which enables them to cope without the organ's overall function deteriorating substantially. To take an example, kidneys can work efficiently with less than 40 per cent of their functional units intact.

If we accept that our dog is beginning to become old at this age, it will encourage us to take early steps towards ensuring a long and fulfilling old age. We can be especially vigilant for signs of geriatric disorders, and try to ensure by good management and provision of the most appropriate diet that we don't precipitate any problems. We should do this even if our dog is still able to run the legs off dogs half his age, still has a juvenile tendency to chew up your slippers, and still manages to convince the opposite sex that he or she is the best looking dog in the park.

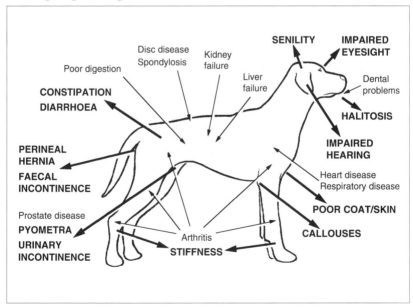

**Figure 1.1.** The signs of an ageing dog

# What are the signs of ageing?

Because of their short life span relative to ours, many of the changes that a dog undergoes throughout its life as well as in old age appear to happen quite suddenly. Puppies seem to change into adults within a few weeks. Similarly thay can appear to decline from dogs in their prime to geriatrics in an equally short time. Of course the process of ageing is actually a gradual one which progresses in fits and starts, and at different rates for different organ systems. Regular observation of our dogs will enable us to spot the changes of old age developing.

### Coat
Greying, of the muzzle initially, is an early sign of ageing. This may happen at quite a young age, four years of age for instance, long before the dog is really a geriatric. It is nevertheless a sign that those hair follicles are showing the effects of old age. The coat will generally become less glossy, and will also thin. The skin may become thickened, darkened and greasy. Callouses and pressure sores may develop over bony prominences such as the elbows.

### Sight
Many dogs develop cloudy lenses in their eyes, which may first become apparent when the light catches the eye in a certain way. True cataracts, which are very dense and white, may also appear. Other ageing processes affect the light-sensitive layers at the back of the eyes (retinas) and these changes may cause the dog to show deteriorating eyesight. This often is first noticeable in poor light, when a dog might bump into lamp posts or look confused when trying to find you when at exercise.

### Hearing
As well as failing eyesight, loss of hearing is common in elderly dogs. This can sometimes appear highly selective as the sound a dog will fail to hear first is his master's voice, and the last thing he will still be able to hear is the rattle of the dinner bowl. There may be a good reason for this since it is likely that the ability to hear different frequencies is lost at different times.

### Muscles and joints
After a life of good service, a dog's muscles and joints are likely to begin to fail. The first sign is usually stiffness on rising in the morning or after a long rest, especially after vigorous exercise.

Joints may be swollen and muscles may be wasted, particularly over the skull, along the back, and from the thighs. As age advances, walking may be slow and stiff, and a dog may limp on one or more limbs.

## Digestion

Your pet may be slower at finishing off her food, or her appetite may decrease so that she leaves part of each meal. Her digestive system may also become more sensitive and bouts of diarrhoea, constipation or vomiting may become more common. Many older dogs will drink more and may be less able to hold their urine (and stools) through the night.

## Disposition

Mentally, older dogs will be more sluggish and less excitable. Owners of Springer Spaniels and the like may have to wait a little longer to detect these symptoms, but they will occur. Ageing dogs are more easily confused by changes in routine and they may become more irritable if disturbed.

# Summary

- **Whatever the causes of ageing and whenever they start to develop in individual animals, there are some basic signs owners can look for so that the 'special care' required by the older dog can start.**

# CHAPTER 2 Diseases of old age

Most diseases can occur at any age, and those that we usually think of as diseases of old age may have started while the dog was relatively young merely becoming more apparent with age. Indeed the majority of diseases that we will cover here can fall into this category.

By being aware of potential problems which can occur later in life, we should be able to observe the early signs of disease so that we can start appropriate treatment as soon as possible. Few of the diseases of old age are curable. In fact, by their very nature they are usually chronic reflecting the irreversible damage to body organs. It is possible however, to slow the progress of disease, so minimising the effect on the quality of life of our canine companions.

## Organ systems

### Musculoskeletal system

#### Arthritis

Perhaps the first image that springs to mind when thinking of an elderly dog is that of a sedate animal which spends much time in its bed. When it rises it is stiff, and when at exercise it is slow and unable to walk very far. It may limp either all the time or only occasionally and affected joints may be swollen and grate when the joint is manipulated. It is an image that we can all sympathise with as the years pass.

Dogs have evolved making great use of their limbs. Wild dogs cover vast distances in search of food, and may run many miles at speed when hunting down prey. Many of our domestic breeds retain this ability. Racing Greyhounds and working Sheepdogs make good use of this talent in the course of their work but even those pet dogs which do not work get much of their life's pleasure from being at exercise.

## The Ageing Dog

A lifetime of use takes it toll on the joints of our dogs, and arthritis is the most common problem of the musculoskeletal system which comes with old age. Joint surfaces are normally covered by smooth protective layer of cartilage, and are bathed by slippery lubricating synovial fluid. Use of the joints over the years rubs away at the cartilage, and the concussion of running and jumping causes further trauma to it. Young animals are able to efficiently repair and maintain this smooth joint surface, but this process becomes less efficient with age. The synovial fluid also becomes thicker and less effective in providing lubrication. The result is roughening of the joint surface which produces inflammation and pain each time the joint is used. Extra bone may also be laid down around the joint in response to the inflammation and although this may not cause continual pain, it disrupts the movement of the joint. Any joints may be affected by arthritis, but some more commonly than others.

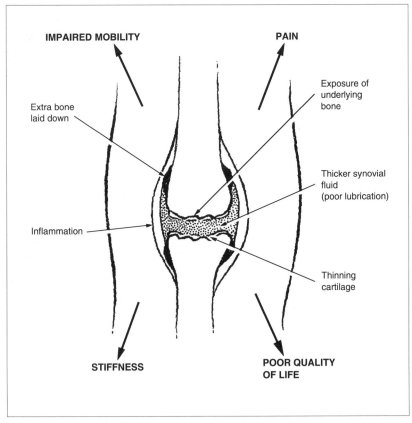

**Figure 2.1** The arthritic joint

The hips are the joints most often affected, which reflects the hard work they perform throughout life and also the fact that many of the larger breeds such as German Shepherd Dogs and Labradors suffer from the condition of hip dysplasia. This is a condition where varying degrees of deformity of the hip joint are present, usually at birth, leading to joint instability and excessive wear and tear so leading to arthritis.

Another disease of young dogs which can give rise to arthritic problems when elderly is osteochondrosis. This is a condition affecting the cartilage of certain joints, particularly the shoulder and, again, affects more commonly the larger breeds . It is also thought to be an important, often undiagnosed, cause of arthritis in the elbow and hock (ankle) later in life.

As well as these diseases of the joints, injuries to the joints throughout life may lead to arthritis in old age. Swift attention to such injuries by way of rest and perhaps medical treatment, and allowing plenty of time for joints to mend before resuming strenuous exercise should help to minimise problems later. If you can see signs of arthritis in your dog, then you can be sure that it is suffering discomfort and some form of treatment should be sought if a reasonable quality of life is to maintained. Modern drugs are effective and safe and taking them is always going to be preferable to having a drug-free, but crippled dog (see later).

Apart from arthritis, several other conditions affect the elderly dog's musculoskeletal system. The spine is subjected to much stress over the years and just as in humans, back pain is a common affliction for older dogs. The discs which separate the vertebrae from each other are particularly vulnerable, deteriorating with age. As a result, a 'slipped disc' is more likely to happen in an aged spine, causing pain, and, if it progresses, affecting the nerve supply to the back legs so that the dog is partially or completely paralysed in the hind legs. The early signs of intervertebral disc disease can be vague. The dog may seem quiet, reluctant to leave its bed or go for a walk, and unwilling to go up steps. If the disc affected is in the neck, the dog may not wish to lower its head to eat or drink. It is quite important at this stage to allow the dog rest if further serious damage is to be prevented. Dogs with long backs, such as dachshunds or basset hounds and those which are overweight are particularly prone to this problem.

Chronic damage of the spinal column may give rise to spondylosis where extra bone is laid down around the vertebrae in response to stress over a long period. This may be painful in its own right, or it may affect the nerves leaving the affected vertebrae, causing weakness of the hind limbs. The symptoms will usually be relieved by the drugs used to treat arthritis, but the condition is progressive, and will worsen, rapidly in some cases, slowly in others.

## Treatment of arthritis

Arthritis, and the signs associated with it, is probably one of the most common conditions of the older dog for which treatment is sought. In addition to the dogs where treatment is actively sought, many other dogs are treated only after presentation to the vet for some other reason such as routine vaccination. A routine health check, usually carried out at that time, may reveal signs of arthritis and it is only after a course of treatment that owners realise how much their dog's mobility had been impaired.

In recent years, several new drugs have been made available for the treatment of the condition in dogs. Whilst the older drugs have been and continue to be very effective in some dogs, these newer drugs seem much better in most cases. These new drugs include those which modify the fluid in the joint and help to heal the joint surface, and members of the non-steroidal anti-inflammatory group of drugs (NSAIDs), such as Zenecarp.

Joint fluid modifiers are thought to assist the repair of the joint surface although response to treatment is usually slow and relief of pain requires improvement in joint surface, a generally slow process.

The NSAIDs provide a much quicker and dependable response because although often thought of as 'just painkillers', they have much wider and more important properties. They provide pain relief by reducing inflammation, often retarding the progression of the disease. The reduction in pain not only improves quality of life, but also allows better joint mobility, so allowing moderate exercise, reducing stiffness and helping to prevent obesity.

Individual dogs may respond differently to the various NSAIDs so that doses can often be considerably reduced while maintaining a therapeutic effect. In addition, just because a dog fails to respond to one NSAID does not mean that it will respond identically to another. Often dogs which have been supposedly maintained on one of the older 'anti-arthritic' drugs show a new lease of life when changed to one of these newer drugs.

Never delay in seeking treatment for arthritis. The changes in your dog will be reward enough.

## Other musculo-skeletal conditions

Old bones are weaker and more brittle so that they are more easily broken and take longer to heal. Rest, good nutrition and attention to body weight are particularly important in elderly dogs recovering from a fracture.

Muscles, too, become weaker with age, as functional muscle cells die and are lost and others become less efficient at using energy sources. Nerve receptors in the muscles may also become less responsive, and damage over the years to the nerve supply of a muscle will lead to the shrinking (atrophy) of that muscle. All these factors contribute to increasing weakness as a dog ages.

Several specific diseases of the nervous supply to muscles can occur. The most common in German Shepherd Dogs is chronic degenerative rediculomyopathy or CDRM. Here the nervous supply to the hind legs is gradually lost, initially causing weakness and occasional loss of footing. The dog will be less aware of the position of its paws, so that it might stand on the backs of the feet. The paws will be dragged causing the tops of the nails to wear away and in its early stages the condition may be confused with arthritis of the hips. The condition will not respond to any treatment and the legs will become progressively paralysed. Although there is no specific treatment for CDRM, much can be done to help an affected dog. As with all conditions of the musculoskeletal system, it is vital that body weight is kept to a minimum (see Chapter 4). Ensure that the surfaces the dog has to walk on indoors give a good grip – carpet rather than linoleum for instance – and keep walks out of the house within the range that the dog can easily manage. Affected dogs are often keen to walk, but will tire easily, and as they tire they drag their hind legs, leading to injuries of the paws. Leather boots can be obtained to protect the paws if this problem is unavoidable.

## In summary

The important rules for conditions of the musculoskeletal system are:

- **Keep the weight down**
- Always exercise within a dog's capabilities – excess strenuous exercise stresses the spine and joints, leading to arthritis and intervertebral disc problems
- Find out why a dog is limping or stiff early on, so that progress of the condition can be halted or slowed if possible
- Get treatment if available – a dog will usually be limping or stiff because it is in discomfort

# Cardiovascular system

Diseases of the cardiovascular system are estimated to affect 25 per cent of dogs aged from 9 – 12, and 33 per cent of dogs 13 and over. This disease may affect the heart and/or the blood vessels.

The most common disorder of the heart in dogs is endocardiosis which is a progressive disease of the inner layer of the heart causing the formation of nodules on the valves. As the nodules grow, the valves of the heart become distorted so that they don't close tightly. This allows backwards leakage of blood which the veterinary surgeon will, quite commonly, hear as a murmur. The dog may show clinical signs of decreased cardiac output and congestive heart failure. Often the first symptom to be noticed is a soft, quiet cough due to fluid collecting in the lungs. A harsher cough may then arise due to the enlargement of the heart causing pressure on the windpipe (trachea). The fluid collecting in the lungs will reduce the dog's capacity for exercise, causing it to pant and cough when ever it exerts itself. As the disease progresses less exertion is necessary to produce symptoms, until eventually the dog will pant even at rest. If the right side of the heart is more affected than the left, then the build up of fluid will be in the abdomen (ascites) rather than the lungs. Reduced cardiac output may reduce the efficiency of many internal organs.

As well as endocardiosis, the loss of heart muscle cells throughout life due to ageing or disease may also impair cardiac function. Areas of heart muscle which have been damaged in life become fibrosed and this may lead to an altered heart rhythm.

The blood vessels supplying heart muscle, like those elsewhere in the body, become more thickened and stiff with age. This leads to a reduction in the oxygen supply to areas of the heart muscle. Blood vessels elsewhere in the body cause an increase in resistance to blood flow which raises blood pressure and puts even more strain on the heart.

Elderly animals will also tend to be anaemic as the rate of red blood cell production slows so reducing the oxygen carrying capacity of the blood, further impairing the cardio-vascular efficiency of the body.

The treatment of heart disease requires control of the dog's diet, exercise and, sometimes, the use of drugs. A low salt diet is essential to reduce the amount of fluid retained in the body so reducing the workload on the heart. See Chapter 8 for more information on nutrition. Obesity puts added strain on the heart and aggravates the

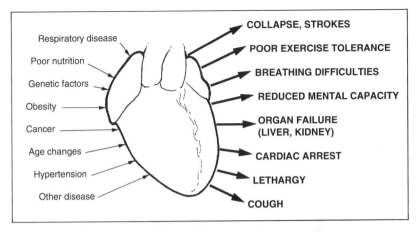

**Figure 2.2** The impact of heart disease on lifestyle

respiratory symptoms by surrounding the airways with fat deposits, so keeping body weight to a minimum is important. If the dog's clinical condition is not too severe, steady exercise should be given. This helps to keep body weight down, increases heart rate, and helps to open up the lung tissue so helping to clear fluid collecting there. The movement of limb muscles helps clear oedema, or excess fluid, which may collect in the legs in the worst cases.

Many different drugs are used to treat cardiac failure. Some encourage the kidneys to lose water so reducing the circulating volume. This reduces the heart's workload and the amount of fluid in the lungs. Other drugs increase the ability of the heart to contract so improving cardiac output or open up airways, so improving respiration and easing the cough often associated with disease. Opening up the blood vessels in the skin and extremities with medication reduces blood pressure, and so the load on the heart and and the rate of beating. This is a common approach to controlling abnormalities of rhythm.

Remember the following in dealing with heart disease:

- Watch out for a cough or excessive panting after exercise
- **Keep the weight down**
- Feed a low salt diet – fresh meat, pasta or potatoes, and vegetables – or use a prescription diet
- Keep up regular gentle exercise if the patient is capable of it
- Seek veterinary attention if you notice any of the symptoms – treatment will improve quality and length of life

# The respiratory system

Respiratory difficulties arise as a result of diseases which affect the heart but in addition, the geriatric lungs become less efficient for other reasons as well.

The cells which produce the secretions of the respiratory system reduce in number, and become less healthy with age and so less, thicker, mucus is secreted. The mucus which in health keeps the airways moist while trapping dust, dirt and bacteria, and the surfactant which prevents the air sacs (alveoli) from collapsing, become less efficient. The tiny hairs on the cells lining the airways which transport inhaled debris up towards the larynx become fewer in number and this combines with the thicker mucus to allow more debris and bacteria to remain in the lungs. Chronic bronchitis is, therefore, a frequent condition in elderly dogs often leading to respiratory infections. Affected animals will cough, they may have difficulty breathing, and if pneumonia sets in, they will be quiet and depressed. As lung tissue becomes older, it also becomes much less elastic so that every time the dog breathes out, he has to actively force air out of his lungs by contracting his respiratory muscles. This involves extra energy and causes additional pressure on the lungs and chest. This makes it even harder for the heart to pump blood to the lungs so further impairing respiratory function. As with other muscles, the respiratory muscles also reduce in size and strength as they age so they are less able to fulfil this new demand, leading to further poor lung function and oxygenation of the blood. This oxygen starvation of the body's tissues speeds the death and reduction in number of cells in all the tissues, including the brain, and accelerates the progress of ageing and senility.

The upper part of the respiratory tract may also be involved in age-related disease. Loss of elasticity of the soft palate in the roof of the mouth, especially in small short-faced breeds, may cause it to droop and cause snoring or gagging. Combined with extra fat laid down around the throat, this can obstruct the airway sufficiently to cause fainting. In large breeds, the vocal cords may become paralysed so that they obstruct the flow of air into the trachea, causing panting and noise on inspiration. This is especially common in Labradors. The lining of the tissues in the nostrils may also become thickened so obstructing the flow of air through the nose particularly if the dog exerts itself. It may also increase susceptibility to infection.

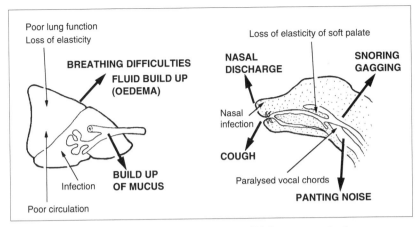

**Figure 2.3** Conditions affecting (a) lung; (b) larynx and pharynx

Treatment of respiratory disease with drugs most commonly involves antibiotics since infections are usually present. Drugs which dilate the airways and help dilute thick mucus are also often used along with steroids and cough suppressants. Treatment of underlying heart disease is also commonly required and surgery may occasionally be an option. The most important aspect of treatment of respiratory diseases is rest which reduces the requirement for oxygen

While respiratory problems in old age may be minor such as a mild cough or snoring, they can lead to serious disruption of lung function and be potentially fatal or contribute to senility by starving important tissues of oxygen. Remember the following points:

- Watch for coughing, harsh panting or reduced exercise tolerance
- Excess weight aggravates or causes several of these problems
- Never let a dog with respiratory symptoms exercise hard
- A dusty or smoky environment leads to bronchial disease in dogs just as in humans

## The digestive system

The geriatric dog's alimentary canal inevitably suffers the ageing process. The older dog, therefore, derives less benefit from its diet so causing an apparent normal or increased appetite accompanied by a loss of weight. This also makes the dog more prone to diarrhoea because poorly digested food in the intestines encourages the multiplication of bacteria which ferment it. This will change the acidity of the bowel contents further favouring growth of further harmful bacteria. A reduction in the amount of mucus being produced in the stomach and saliva being swallowed, as a result of the salivary glands becoming infiltrated with fat, means that the stomach may be more prone to ulceration. Any degree of kidney failure results in a higher level of urea in the blood and this is another important cause of stomach ulcers. Ulcers cause discomfort and vomiting with dark spots of partially digested blood appearing in the vomit.

The nerve supply to the gullet (oesophagus) may also be impaired so reducing the coordination and strength of the gullet. This slows the passage of food to the stomach and may cause regurgitation of food or indigestion.

At the other end, a tendency in older dogs to be dehydrated because of deteriorating kidneys increases the incidence of constipation leading to poor appetite, vomiting, malaise and abdominal discomfort. This usually causes dogs to strain and make several unsuccessful attempts to defecate.

Inflammation of the large intestine, colon and rectum may also cause frequent attempts to defecate, accompanied by straining. The dog may produce only small amounts of stools, often loose, containing blood and covered in mucus. This may be caused by chronic inflammation initiated by an acute bout of diarrhoea which leaves the old dog's more susceptible large bowel irritated. Benign growths or polyps are another common problem in the bowel of the older dog which may cause these symptoms.

Anal sacs or anal glands (scent glands located on either side of the anus) are a regular cause of problems in the older dog. The secretion which

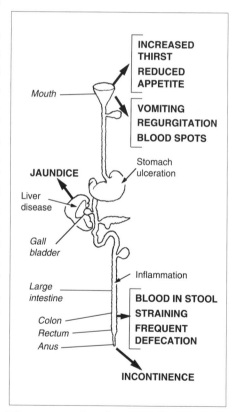

**Figure 2.4** Conditions affecting the digestive tract

should be evacuated each time the dog passes a stool, becomes thicker and less easily expressed. Irregular bowel movements, and reduced bulk of the stools, both problems of geriatrics, further reduce the efficiency of emptying the sacs. When the sacs are impacted, or overfull, they cause discomfort and are liable to become infected. Affected dogs may rub their bottoms along the ground, show signs of straining to pass faeces or bite at the base of the tail or flanks or even their paws in an attempt to relieve the irritation

The liver is an important part of the digestive system which also suffers the wear and tear of age. Like other organs, the aged liver has fewer, less efficient, functional cells, and although, unlike other major organs, it has a great capacity for regeneration, as old age progresses, damage earlier in life starts to take its toll. The liver may suffer from cirrhosis which is a destructive fibrosis and scarring of the organ which reduces the amount of useful liver available. Bile, produced by the liver, emulsifies fats to allow their digestion, and neutralises stomach acid. When less bile is secreted into the bowel by the failing liver, fat digestion is impaired and ulcers of the duodenum are more common because of stomach acid spilling over. As well as secreting bile to aid digestion, the liver receives all the nutrients produced by the act of digestion and processes them before distributing them around the body or storing them. It is also essential for the detoxification of materials such as ammonia (produced in the alimentary canal as a by-product of protein digestion) or drugs. Liver disease of old age may therefore lead to a build up of toxic materials in the body. It may also give rise to increased thirst, vomiting, reduced appetite, an appetite for unusual things, swollen abdomen, weight loss, jaundice (may be seen in the whites of the eyes) or merely lethargy or vague illness.

Much of the care of an elderly dog's digestive system relates to diet, and will be covered in more detail in the chapter on nutrition. Encouraging regular defecation by exercising is helpful in regulating bowel function, and allowing plenty of opportunity will help control another geriatric problem – incontinence of the bowel.

Key points relating to geriatric digestive problems:

- Observe your pet – watch for straining or unusual faeces
- Seek advice if your dog vomits several times in one day, or daily on a regular basis
- Feed an easily digested, low bulk diet
- Consider food supplements – fibre, vitamins, minerals and others
- Avoid treats such as chocolate, spicy meats, curry.

## The urinary system

Chronic kidney failure is a common disease of old age. The kidneys are particularly vulnerable to the ageing process because the cells which die throughout life are not replaced so that the amount of healthy kidney tissue is constantly reducing. A young dog suffering from a viral or bacterial illness affecting the kidneys may appear to make a full recovery, but the cells lost at that time will be missed later in life. Despite this however, the kidneys are able to lose much of their mass (up to 60 per cent) before signs of disease become evident. The main function of the kidneys is to filter and clean the blood, disposing of toxins and waste material in the urine, and at the same time regulating water loss from the body. When the kidneys start to fail, excess water is lost, so that the dog will pass more urine and drink more water to compensate. Useful materials such as proteins are also lost into the urine, and this contributes to weight loss in many old dogs. At the same time waste materials such as urea, a breakdown product of protein metabolism, which are normally excreted into the urine, are retained. High blood levels of these waste materials may cause bleeding and ulceration in the gut, mouth and tongue, the smell of urine on the breath, vomiting, anaemia, lethargy and incoordination, fits or coma.

Treatment of kidney failure with anabolic steroids may slow the rate of tissue loss and stimulate the remaining tissue to work more effectively. We can also reduce the kidneys' work load by feeding a more appropriate diet which will be described in more detail in Chapter 8.

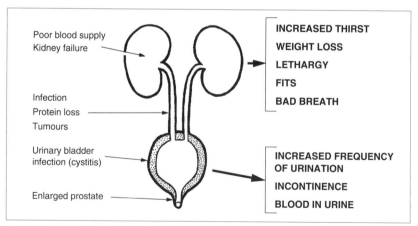

**Figure 2.5** Conditions affecting the urinary system

The other part of the urinary system which frequently develops problems in old age is the bladder. A weakening of the muscles of the wall of the bladder means that urine is not always completely emptied from the bladder. This can lead to chronic infection of the bladder (cystitis) which may flare up from time to time as bouts of acute cystitis. These are seen as frequent attempts to pass water which often contains blood and may lead to incontinence, a common affliction of old-age, particularly in the bitch.

Incontinence may also arise due to an increase in urine production, maybe as a result of kidney failure or some other cause. This may mean that the old dog simply can't make it through the night. Weakness of the sphincter muscle in the neck of the bladder, due to its ageing or due to hormonal imbalance, is another cause. Mental senility will also reduce bladder control. Obesity, whilst not a cause, is also an important factor so that often, if an affected bitch can successfully lose weight, the condition may resolve.

Treatment of incontinence will depend on the cause but may consist of antibiotics to treat cystitis, oestrogen for hormone replacement therapy, or drugs which improve the tone of the bladder neck sphincter as necessary. Reasons for increased urine production will need to be investigated, as kidney failure is only one of many. Liver disease, diabetes mellitus and psychological factors are all causes of excessive drinking and so may, indirectly lead to incontinence. Trying to control nocturnal incontinence by restricting water in the evening is only safe if the increased thirst is not due to a medical problem and veterinary advice should be sought.

Points about the recognition and care of urinary system disorders:

- Watch for increased thirst and urine production, vomiting, bad breath, incontinence and weight loss
- Feed a diet low in protein, but of good nutritional value – prescription diets are available
- Supplement with B vitamins
- Allow unrestricted access to water
- Give antacids, such as aluminium hydroxide, to reduce stomach ulceration

## The reproductive system

Old dogs continue to be sexually capable throughout their lives, although their levels of sex hormones become much reduced. Male dogs undergo a steady reduction in sex drive and interest as they age, although there are exceptions to the rule! Bitches do not undergo the menopause but continue to have seasons although they may become less frequent and less obvious with age. As time goes by, seasons are less likely to be a source of nuisance to owners, and more likely to be a health risk to bitches.

## Bitches

Throughout life, a bitch's ovaries secrete progesterone (the hormone which maintains pregnancy) after each season, for up to two months, whether mated or not. In response to this, the walls of the womb thicken and fluid is secreted in preparation for implantation of the embryos and carrying of foetuses. With successive seasons, the effects on the womb become more significant so that it may eventually become more prone to infection. By the time a bitch is 8 years old, many will be undergoing some degree of womb infection after each season and whilst this may be minor at first, it can become serious and even life-threatening. The womb may become pus-filled in a condition called pyometra. A bitch affected with a pyometra may:

- be off colour a few weeks after the end of her season
- have increased thirst
- vomit
- sometimes show lameness in the hind limbs
- show purulent vaginal discharge

Although bitches may respond to antibiotics, response is usually only temporary and the condition may recur after the end of treatment or after subsequent seasons. Surgery to remove the infected womb is usually the only satisfactory cure. In many cases the patient is very sick as a result of the toxic effects of bacteria in the womb so she may be more sensitive to anaesthetic agents. Despite this, the success rate is usually good.

The mammary glands of ageing bitches are very prone to develop lumps and 60 per cent of unspayed bitches will be affected by the time they are 11 years old. These may be fibrous masses or tumours. Cancer of the mammary glands is very common is unspayed bitches, and makes up 25 per cent of all cancer in bitches. Because it is not possible to tell whether lumps in the mammary glands are benign or malignant except by laboratory analysis, and because malignancies are common, early veterinary advice should be sought as soon as any lumps are felt. The earlier tumours are removed, the less likely they are to spread.

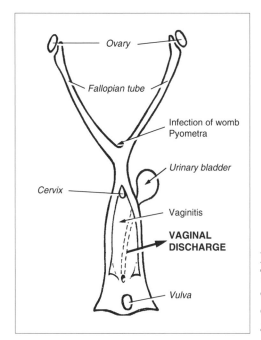

**Figure 2.6**
The reproductive organs of the bitch and the conditions which may affect them.

Spaying a bitch when young dramatically reduces the chances of mammary cancer developing. If a bitch is spayed after her first season, then the incidence of tumours is reduced by 95 per cent. This protecting effect diminishes with each subsequent season. This benefit and the elimination of risk regarding the occurrence of pyometra, are very strong arguments for the spaying of bitches early in life.

Points to consider about the female reproductive system:

- Watch for signs of illness in the two months following a season – vomiting, increased thirst, lameness, vaginal discharge, loss of appetite or generally 'off colour'
- Look out for lumps in mammary glands and around the anus

## Male dog

Like bitches, elderly entire male dogs are not free from reproductive problems in old age. Under the influence of the hormone testosterone, the prostate gland tends to become enlarged with age and so is at risk of infection, abscesses, cysts, or cancer. The enlarged or diseased gland may cause the following symptoms:

- difficulty in passing stools
- the stools may be compressed ('ribbon faeces')
- difficulty in passing urine (only a dribble may be produced)
- increased frequency of urination
- blood dripping from the penis
- a pussy discharge from the prepuce
- pain in the abdomen
- hind limb lameness

Treatment of simple hormonally induced prostate enlargement will involve either hormonal treatment to counteract the effects of testosterone on the gland, or castration to remove the source of the testosterone. Castration is the only permanent treatment, as the condition will recur as soon as any hormonal therapy is stopped. Additionally antibiotics and pain killers may be necessary.

Another common disease of elderly dogs is testicular cancer which may occur in as many as 60 per cent of male dogs particularly where a testicle is retained. Affected dogs will usually have an enlarged testicle, which may or may not be painful and since many testicular tumours involve cells which secrete oestrogen, feminisation may occur. This causes the prepuce to be droopy, and the skin and hair covering to be poor. Because of the effects of the oestrogen, the other testicle will usually be abnormally small, accentuating the difference between it and the cancerous testicle.

Another type of tumour which it is worth mentioning here is the perianal adenoma. Although not affecting the reproductive system, they do grow in response to testosterone, and are a common tumour of elderly male dogs. They occur around the anus, between the anus and the scrotum, and under the base of the tail. Initially they are small lumps under the skin, but as they enlarge they will become ulcerated and bleed. Once present they need to be removed surgically, but castration will greatly reduce the chances of new ones developing.

Entire male dogs are also at risk from perineal hernias. Due to the effects of male hormones, the muscles on either side of the rectum and anus atrophy and rupture. This can allow a hernia to develop. The signs will vary depending on which internal tissues enter the hernia. A swelling on one side of the anus will be obvious and is often tender to the touch. If the rectum deviates into the hernia, the dog will show signs of constipation and the straining may lead to some blood being passed in the stools. If the bladder passes into the hernia, the dog may have difficulty urinating or may be unable to do so at all.

Treatment of a perineal hernia will depend on the symptoms. A mild case with constipation may respond to stool softeners and a controlled diet. A dog with a herniated bladder will need urgent attention to relieve the obstruction to urine flow.

Surgery is often necessary to correct the hernia, but unfortunately because repair is difficult, breakdown is quite common. Castration is often carried out to try to reduce the chances of recurrence, either of the original hernia or of a hernia on the other side.

Points to consider about the male reproductive system:

- Look out for lumps in testicles and around the anus
- With old male dogs, watch for difficulty in passing water, incontinence, or blood or pus discharging from the penis
- Look for signs of a perineal hernia in male dogs – swelling on one side of the anus, constipation, difficulty in passing urine.
- Be aware of the benefits of neutering – this section is almost unnecessary for owners of neutered animals
- Don't be worried about having an elderly dog neutered, especially if it develops any of these problems – many owners of elderly dogs which are spayed or castrated report a new lease of life

## The endocrine (hormonal) system

Hormones play an important role in the regulation of body function. They are best described as chemical messengers, which are secreted into the blood from glands, to act on tissues in locations distant from their source. Some of these hormones secreted by one gland, act on other unrelated glands to regulate production of the second glands own hormones. Examples of hormones are insulin, thyroxin, cortisone and the sex hormones.

Whilst most hormonal diseases can occur in dogs of any age, most hormones are secreted in lower amounts as dogs age. Thyroxin, for example, the hormone secreted by the thyroid gland, is secreted in smaller quantities in older animals. This hormone is extremely important in regulating the rate of body metabolism and the reduced levels seen in older dogs are important in contributing to the ageing process. Lower levels of thyroid hormone cause lethargy, weight gain and poor skin and coat quality. In the worst cases, these signs will be obvious but in an old dog with gradually reducing thyroid function, these signs may be more subtle and just taken for granted as signs of 'old age'. Sometimes supplementation of thyroid hormone can be useful to improve the general symptoms of ageing.

# The Ageing Dog

Diabetes mellitus tends to affect middle aged to elderly dogs. This disease is relatively common and results from a reduction in the secretion of insulin, the hormone which regulates glucose metabolism. This gives rise to an increase in urine production and, to compensate, an increase in thirst. At the same time, glucose is lost in the urine with insufficient glucose being made available to body tissues thus giving rise to weakness and loss of weight. A classic sign of this condition is the formation of cataracts in the eyes. (For more information on this condition please see *The Management of Diabetes Mellitus* by Mr J W Simpson MRCVS – Henston Ltd). The treatment of diabetes is usually very successful, but is complex and involves much commitment from an owner.

Another hormonal disorder common in middle aged to older dogs which causes an increased thirst is Cushing's Syndrome caused by an increase in the levels of cortisone, secreted by the adrenal gland. The main symptoms of Cushing's Syndrome are increased thirst and urine production, increased appetite, weakness and loss of muscle mass, swollen abdomen, thin coat, especially on the flanks, and soft skin, which may be darkened in colour. Treatment of Cushing's Syndrome depends on the initial cause and is often complicated.

The sex hormones can cause several disorders which have been discussed above but in addition, falling levels of testosterone speeds the ageing process, since its action is as an anabolic steroid which encourages muscle growth and function. Low levels of sex hormones weaken the muscles, allow weight loss, and cause a slowing down of mental function.

Key points regarding hormonal disorders:

- These are an important cause of increased thirst and urine production
- Affected dogs may become incontinent
- Watch for increased appetite, especially if weight is lost
- Hair loss and skin changes are common signs
- The changes come on gradually, so it is important to be aware of them and seek advice if any are noticed
- Hormonal imbalances are an important cause of many of the signs of ageing

## The immune system

The body has a very active defence mechanism which acts to protect the body by eliminating bacteria or virus infections which threaten it. As a dog ages, these various defence mechanisms become impaired. The decline in the immune system occurs alongside a reduction in the protection afforded by physical defences. For example, as we have seen, the skin, respiratory system, bladder and other organs are all less able to prevent bacteria from invading them. This all means that geriatric dogs are more likely to suffer infections, and when contracted, these infections are more likely to develop into serious conditions.

In order to minimise these risks, it is important to ensure vaccinations are up to date. In addition, elderly dogs should not be exposed unnecessarily to situations where infectious diseases are more likely (in kennels for example) and they should only be so exposed when in the best of health. It is especially vital to seek prompt attention for any illness and to provide a healthy diet and comfortable environment.

Key points about the immune system:

- It is important to ensure vaccinations are up to date
- Elderly dogs can be more susceptible to infections and disease
- Seek early treatment for any illness, and follow that treatment through until the dog is completely cured
- The healthier the dog, the better its immune system, so the right diet and environment are important

# Body parts affected by disease

## The mouth and teeth

Dental disease is without doubt the most common disorder of elderly dogs. Even by the age of 3 it is estimated that 80 per cent of dogs require some form of dental treatment, and by the time a dog is geriatric it is almost certain to have a significant degree of dental disease. This can range from small amounts of tartar on the teeth and gingivitis to massive chunks of scale hiding whole teeth and raging infections of the gums and teeth roots.

Dental disease is also perhaps the most underestimated of conditions affecting the older dog. To start with it is often not noticed. Unless an effort is made to examine the teeth and gums, their condition may remain a mystery. Even when the mouth is examined and the state of the teeth is seen, we fail to appreciate how profoundly it affects the health of our pet. The signs of dental disease are:

- halitosis (bad breath)
- reluctance to chew, or awkwardness when eating
- loss of appetite
- salivation
- swelling of a cheek, caused by a root abscess
- general loss of condition
- bouts of vomiting

On lifting the gums and examining the mouth, you may see:

- brown scale on the teeth
- red, sore gums
- bleeding from the gums
- pus discharging from the root sockets
- broken teeth
- missing teeth
- loose teeth

Dental disease in our dogs stems partly from breeding, and partly from the diet which we feed them. Small breeds of dog, especially those with short faces, have jaws crowded with teeth. Food becomes lodged between them, encouraging plaque, bacterial growth and gum infection. Small breeds also tend to eat a softer diet than the larger breeds, which doesn't help natural cleaning processes.

In the natural state, dogs must bite and chew through hide, fur and feathers to reach their food. They also tend to chew the bones of carcasses. This all has an excellent abrasive action which keeps teeth scraped clean. Our dogs tend to eat a relatively soft diet, with food which not only sticks to the teeth, but has little cleaning value. All the advantage doesn't lie with the natural diet, however. Wild dogs' teeth often crack on bones, reducing their value to the animal, and allowing root abscesses to develop. Their teeth will also wear down gradually, and loss of functioning teeth is a major cause of death in wild carnivores. Our pets have the advantage that their teeth, if well cared for, will last much longer, and even if all their teeth are extracted or fall out, they will still be able to eat the soft diet we feed them.

## Plaque and infections
When food sticks to the teeth, it allows plaque to develop. Plaque is a layer of bacteria feeding on the food, and secreting chemicals which

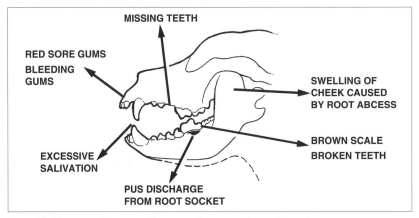

**Figure 2.7** Conditions affecting the mouth and teeth

damage the enamel. If this plaque is not cleaned away, it becomes calcified by the minerals in saliva. This tartar has a much rougher surface than enamel, and provides a good home for more bacteria. The mineralisation continues, and eventually the tooth may disappear under a shell of tartar.

Tartar which develops along the gum line pushes the gums back from the crown of the tooth, and the bacteria on the tooth surface encourage this gum recession, and also infect the space between the gum and tooth. This infection loosens the tooth in its socket, and may cause root abscesses. Halitosis is an early sign caused by the smell released by bacterial activity.

Gum infection and inflammation, gingivitis, is painful at all stages of the disease whether the gums are just reddened or if the condition has reached the stage when pus is leaking from the tooth/gum junction. When the infection tracks down the root, it become painful to place any pressure on the tooth, for instance when biting or chewing. The lumps of tartar themselves may become large enough to cause discomfort themselves, and they often cause ulcers on cheeks or tongue where they rub up against them.

## General health

If dogs are afflicted with painful mouths, their general health suffers. They will be reluctant to groom and the discomfort their teeth cause will give rise to general lethargy and loss of condition. Geriatric animals are less well able to go without food than younger dogs and any inability to eat will cause a degree of starvation which may precipitate other problems, such as liver and kidney failure.

The large quantities of bacteria collecting in the mouth may lead to infections of the throat and tonsils or gastro-intestinal upsets when swallowed. The bacteria may also enter the bloodstream and be carried to other sites, such as the lungs, heart and kidneys causing other serious infections. Untreated dental disease can therefore have diverse detrimental effects.

## Prevention and treatment

The most important step towards avoiding serious dental disease is observation. Be aware of the condition of your dog's mouth. If the dog has a regular veterinary check up, at booster vaccinations for instance, the vet will look at its teeth and advise accordingly. Regular cleaning is extremely helpful, and this is covered in Chapter 6. Imagine the state our own mouths would be in if we never brushed our teeth. It is only sensible that the same should apply to dogs' teeth.

Treatment of dental disease and its consequences may simply require the use of antibiotics but often it is necessary to remove tartar and to smooth off the enamel to leave a surface which will discourage the attachment of fresh plaque. A general anaesthetic is usually necessary to allow mechanical scaling of the teeth and polishing afterwards although occasionally it is possible to crack off large pieces of tartar while the dog is conscious. The fact that an aged dog has to undergo a general anaesthetic to have its teeth cleaned often puts owners off but they should not make the mistake of seeing this as a purely cosmetic operation. Dental care makes a major contribution towards the health, well being and comfort of geriatric dogs, and unless there is a valid health reason for avoiding the anaesthetic, the great benefits of the treatment far outweigh its relatively minor risks.

Other types of dental disease include cracked or worn teeth in dogs which chew stones. This can lead to extremely painful teeth and when the sensitive tissues in the middle of the tooth, the pulp, become exposed, infections can enter. Veterinary surgeons are often now equipped to perform many of the procedures which your own dentist would carry out, from fillings to root canal treatments, so that if these disorders are seen early enough it is possible to preserve the affected teeth rather than simply removing them.

**Remember:**
- Examine your dog's mouth regularly
- Dental treatment is **not** simply cosmetic – it is vital to your dog's health and well-being

- Feed a healthy diet – some hard material should be included if tinned meat is fed
- Don't give sweet treats
- Encourage chewing, but not bones and stones
- Carry out a teeth cleaning programme at home
- When considering whether dental treatment is necessary, try to imagine how your mouth might feel if affected by the tartar and gingivitis that many dogs suffer

## The eyes

Deteriorating eyesight is common in old dogs. This comes about because of changes affecting all parts of the eye. The lenses will often start to appear blue in colour, and become more opaque as the dog ages. This is not due to cataracts, but a condition called nuclear sclerosis which results from an increased density of the fibres in the lens. Dogs can usually see quite adequately through these lenses, although vision will be slightly impaired, especially in situations of poor light. As the condition progresses, eventually most vision will be lost.

### Cataracts

True cataracts, which are whiter and denser in nature, are relatively common. They may arise as a result of metabolic disease, such as diabetes mellitus, or poisoning, or through other factors. Dogs affected with cataracts may become totally blind although it is possible to

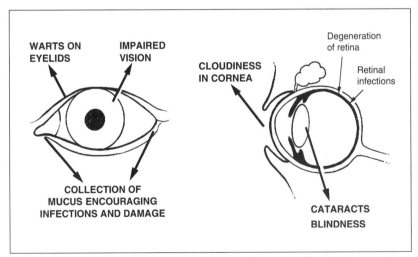

**Figure 2.8** Conditions affecting the eye (a) externally; (b) internally

29

operate to remove the affected lens as long as the rest of the eye is healthy, thus restoring a measure of vision.

## Loss of sight

Dogs will also become blind through degeneration of the retina. There are varied reasons for this. Simple age changes may be responsible although some breeds such as Labradors and Golden Retrievers suffer from hereditary retinal diseases such as progressive retinal atrophy (PRA). Some infections may also cause damage to the retina.

Because dogs don't rely on their vision to the same extent that we do, the loss of their sight need not be a disaster. Smell and hearing are at least as important senses to a dog and owners are sometimes surprised to find that their dogs have lost their vision, so well do they cope. Once a dog has come to terms with the fact that it can't see, it can lead a very active and happy life. It will be confident around the home as long as furniture is not moved, and will also be able to cope with walks along familiar routes. The main concern is that they may be unaware of dangers such as cars approaching, and we will need to be vigilant on their behalf.

## Other signs to watch for

The tears secreted by an old dog will tend to be thicker than those of a young animal and they may not lubricate and clean the eyes as well as they used to. The eyes may therefore be more prone to infections and, more seriously, ulcers. Mucus may tend to collect in the corners of the eyes, especially overnight. Cleaning the eyes, and bathing them with cooled boiled water is helpful in improving comfort and preventing infections and other, more serious, eye damage. Liquid tear replacement drops may be prescribed by your veterinary surgeon if this is a problem.

Warts on the eyelids are very common in elderly dogs, growing from glands along the edges of the eyelids. They should be checked by a veterinary surgeon and, since some may grow until they rub against the surface of the eye causing ulceration and infection, they may need to be removed if the dog is a suitable candidate for general anaesthesia.

Key points about the eyes:

- Watch for cloudiness in the eyes (lenses or corneas), discharges from the eyes, warts on the eyelids

- Seek treatment or advice early – eye disorders can be very painful, and can progress rapidly, putting the eye at risk of permanent damage
- Failing eyesight is common
- Blindness is not necessarily a serious disability for dogs
- Elderly eyes need to be cleaned and cared for

# The ears

Loss of hearing will affect almost all dogs to a greater or lesser extent when they age. This is partly due to ageing effects on the hearing apparatus in the inner ear but it may also be a aggravated by disease in the ear canal. The secretions of the ear canal change with age, and wax tends to accumulate more readily. This will reduce the hearing sensitivity by the physical obstruction itself, but it may also cause inflammatory disease and infection of the ear canal, further reducing hearing. If a dog has suffered repeated ear infections during its younger life, the walls of the ear canals will be thickened, thus reducing the passage of sound to the eardrum or indeed the eardrum itself may be thickened and thus a poorer conductor of sound.

### Infections

As well as reducing hearing ability, ear infections are a source of great irritation and pain to a dog and so it is important to seek prompt attention for any ear conditions. The longer an ear infection is left before treatment, the longer it will take to cure, and if left too long, a complete cure may become unlikely.

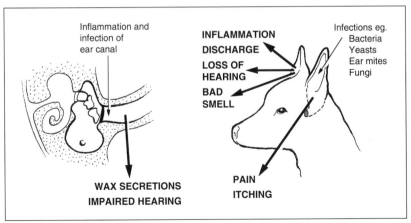

**Figure 2.9** Conditions affecting the ear (a) the middle and inner ear; (b) the external ear

Treatment of ear infections will usually involve cleaning the ear canal and applying drops or ointments containing antibiotics, anti-fungal agents and anti-inflammatory drugs. In worse cases, systemic treatment may also be needed or in the worst cases, your veterinary surgeon may suggest surgery to remove part of the ear canal to improve ventilation of the ear and to allow drainage of discharges and easy access for treatment.

### Prevention

Cleaning an elderly dog's ears regularly will cut down the build up of wax, help to prevent the build up of bacteria, yeasts and ear mites, and enable you to see the early signs of an ear infection such as an increase in wax, redness, smell, or sensitivity of the ear canal. You should also look out for excessive scratching of the ear, shaking the head or holding the head to one side.

### Remember:

- Watch for the signs above
- Seek early treatment for ear infections – they rarely if ever get better on their own
- It is not safe to use home remedies – the ear must be examined thoroughly before treatment is given, and the right treatment must be used
- Don't be tempted to use old medicines – they go off, you may be building up a resistant population of bacteria and yeasts, and a complete course of treatment must be used to ensure that a chronic problem doesn't develop
- Do clean ears regularly, but don't put any disinfectants, soaps or powders down a dog's ear – use a proprietary ear cleaner
- Take care not to startle deaf dogs, and watch for dangerous situations, near roads for instance

## The skin

The geriatric dog's skin will be markedly changed from that of the young dog. The skin is less elastic, the skin secretions change in nature and greasy, somewhat smelly, skin is common. Flakiness is also common. Calluses may develop at pressure points such as the elbows and these, and indeed all the skin, may be more prone to infections, more easily damaged and take longer to heal. The coat is thinner and bald patches and greyness may develop. The claws may be longer through less exercising and become more brittle and grow in a deformed manner.

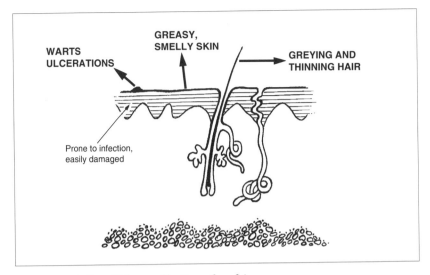

**Figure 2.10** Conditions affecting the skin

Warts are common on the skin of elderly dogs and occur most often around the head and on the legs. Unlike warts on the eyelids, normally they are best left alone unless they are very large, are in a particularly unsightly place, annoy the dog or become ulcerated. In these cases they can be surgically removed. Human wart treatments are not usually effective on canine warts.

It is important to improve and maintain the condition of the elderly dog's skin and coat. Regular grooming helps and bathing may be helpful in decreasing greasiness and removing flakes of dead skin. Shampoos may remove useful as well as unpleasant oils from the skin, so bathing should not be overdone. Special mild shampoos, and shampoos for treating various specific skin conditions are available. Nutritional supplements containing essential fatty acids are also useful in improving skin condition, and protecting against the inflammatory effects of allergies and infections. Calluses can be softened by using hand cream or baby oil, and should be cleaned and bathed if they become damaged or grazed. Providing suitable bedding will reduce the tendency for them to form.

Key points about the skin:

- Watch for increased greasiness, dandruff, loss of coat, calluses, warts and skin infections
- More attention to grooming and cleaning is required as a dog ages
- Nutritional supplements are very helpful in maintaining or improving skin and coat condition

# Tumours and cancer

I mention cancer last and as a separate entity, because it affects any body system, and produces many of the symptoms that we have covered. Cancer is the single most common cause of death in dogs.

It is not always known why a particular tumour may grow, or why they are more common in certain organs. Nor is it always known why certain tumours are more common in particular breeds of dog. A good deal is understood, however, and with each year, advances in human and veterinary medicine reveal more.

Tumours consist of collections of abnormal cells which may develop through the action of a virus, in response to carcinogenic chemicals, or the effects of hormones on tissues making them more prone to developing tumours. Abnormal cells may also arise as a result of mutations which occur spontaneously, the rate of which may be enhanced by carcinogens such as those mentioned above or radiation. The rate of these mutations also increases as cells age.

Many of these mutations are benign and simply die away. Some are more sinister and reproduce themselves rapidly until a tumour is formed. Some of these tumours will be benign, in that they do not spread to other sites, and have limited effects on the dog. Others may be malignant to some degree, spreading seeds to other sites, and/or producing profound effects on the dog by destroying useful tissue in organs. Tumours may also affect the host by secreting hormones or chemicals. The most common tumour of the testicles in dogs, for example, is called a Sertoli cell tumour, and its cells secrete oestrogen, which can produce profound feminising effects on the dog.

Old dogs are more likely to suffer from tumours because:

- Old cells produce more frequent mutations
- Carcinogens have had more time to work upon the dogs' tissues
- The longer a dog lives, the more likely it is that one or more of its mutations will develop into cancer

The most common tumours in all dogs are skin growths. About 30 per cent of these are malignant. They are by far the tumours most frequently reported by dog owners because they are the most obvious. For the same reason they are reported at an earlier stage than other types of tumour, and this gives the opportunity for early treatment. Mammary tumours in unspayed bitches are also very common as are tumours of the testicles and the prostate gland in males.

Malignant tumours, wherever they arise, will spread to other organs and those most commonly affected by secondary tumours are the lungs, liver and kidneys.

## Treatment

When an old animal is ill, cancer will be one of the causes that the veterinary surgeon will consider. If treatment is possible, it is best to carry it out as rapidly as possible both to prevent spread of the tumour, and because early treatment always gives the best chance of success. The most common treatment for cancer in dogs, and the most successful, is surgery to remove the tumour. It is worth repeating that early surgery is the best approach. Owners are often reluctant to commit their dog to general anaesthetic, preferring a wait and see approach. This is wrong for the following reasons:

- Until a tumour is removed, a veterinary surgeon will rarely be able to diagnose which type it is – by waiting until a tumour enlarges before removing it, opportunity is given for the tumour to spread elsewhere
- Malignant tumours can remain small for some time before suddenly growing – when this happens they are at their most malignant, so removal before they grow offers the best chance of complete cure, with no spreading or regrowth of the tumour
- Removal of a small tumour means a shorter anaesthetic, a smaller wound and a more rapid recovery for the patient
- Although it is right to be concerned about subjecting an elderly dog to a general anaesthetic, if a tumour subsequently develops to the point where it needs surgery, the dog will be that much older, and have to have a longer anaesthetic into the bargain
- If a tumour is left to grow for too long it may not be possible to surgically remove it, either because there isn't enough skin at the site to repair the wound, or because it has infiltrated around vital structures

When a tumour is removed, the veterinary surgeon may offer to have it sent to a pathologist to identify it. This helps by giving some idea of the eventual outcome of the cancer, and by enabling future treatment to be planned.

Chemotherapy is another method of treatment, sometimes used as well as surgery. This method of treatment is in its infancy as far as veterinary medicine is concerned, but for the right type of cancer good results can be obtained. It is rare to cure cancer by chemotherapy alone, but the disease can sometimes be slowed or halted. The mention of chemotherapy often conjures up images of the side effects suffered by people undergoing this type of treatment although much of the treatment used in dogs has much milder, if any, side effects. Radiotherapy is also used in veterinary medicine, although most vets will need to refer patients for such treatment.

It should also be remembered that it is possible to reduce the incidence of tumours by preventive measures. Spaying of bitches when young dramatically reduces the incidence of malignant mammary cancer. Castration of males will nearly eliminate prostatic growths, and will entirely eliminate testicular cancer, as well as greatly reducing the incidence of perianal adenomas.

# Summary

- Cancer is very common in old dogs
- Cancer is the single most common cause of death
- Cancer can occur in any organ system, and cause virtually any symptoms
- Early removal of tumours is better for the dogs, and may save lives
- Delaying treatment is dangerous for the health of the dog
- Although cancer is common, most lumps and bumps found on dogs will be benign, so seek a professional opinion early, but don't worry yourself unnecessarily.

# CHAPTER 3 Behavioural aspects of old age

As a dog ages, its mental health can deteriorate just as its physical health can. Some of these changes are a result of the physical ageing of the brain which causes a loss of functioning neurones. This is irreversible. Other changes in behaviour are a result of the physical effects of ageing on other body systems, some of which can be modified or eliminated by attending to the physical problems, or by making allowances and taking them into consideration.

## Character changes

Most dogs will undergo some changes in character as they age. As they become less able to exercise, they will tend to sleep for a greater proportion of the day. This sleep may be deeper, partly because of impaired hearing, but also because they are generally less alert and less able to rouse themselves. In general, there is no problem with this and elderly dogs should be allowed to sleep as long as they wish. Care should be taken when disturbing them as they may be surprised and confused as they awake. This may cause them to snap without really meaning to. This is particularly important when there are young children about who may want to wake the dogs unknown to the owner in the hopes of play.

### Avoiding lethargy
Several diseases of old age, such as arthritis, heart failure and liver disease, will make a dog lethargic and successful treatment for these will often improve general alertness and give the dog more energy.

Although plenty of rest should be allowed to an old dog, the reason for apparent lethargy may be due not to mental deterioration or other physical ailments but simply to a lack of stimulation and boredom.

As the dog becomes physically weaker, it may be taken out for exercise less frequently and for shorter periods. It may be felt that it is less able to take part in family outings and activities and so misses out on these forms of stimulation. It is therefore important to maintain some form of stimulation if an ever declining spiral of lethargy is to be avoided.

Older dogs should be offered more frequent, short walks – even if they are just around the garden – rather than the longer ones he may have been used to.

Daily grooming and time just spent stroking and petting provide useful stimuli and may stave off boredom. Meals given in two or three small portions throughout the day are not only good for other body systems such as stomach and bowels but this also provides additional highlights and regular stimulus. Take the dog out whenever possible even if not specifically for exercise. A ride to the shops in the car, for example, is to be recommended whenever possible as long as they are able to get in and out of the car without excess strain. Introducing another dog may also provide additional, welcomed stimuli.

## Temper

Older dogs are usually thought of as more grumpy than their younger counterparts. This may stem from frustration and discomfort. Many geriatric dogs suffer with arthritis, and the constant discomfort that this can bring may make them intolerant of people and other dogs. The improvement in temper seen in some old dogs when they are put on suitable treatment can be dramatic. The frustration felt when old limbs and an old heart make a dog unable to keep up with a younger animal can also show itself as bad temper.

Failing hearing and eyesight may reduce a dog's sense of security, and allow it to be surprised, especially by children and youthful dogs. This will often make it aggressive in an attempt at defence and it is important to bear this in mind and ensure that an elderly dog isn't bothered by children.

Old dogs often become reluctant to allow their owners to interfere with them. They may growl when they have their ears examined, or their claws clipped or when they are groomed. As before, this may be due to discomfort or insecurity, or it may, in contrast, be because the dog has learned what it has to put up with and what it needn't suffer. An increase in self-confidence which comes with age can make a dog as cantankerous as anything else.

# Senility

Some changes in a dog's behaviour as it ages are not attributable to physical disorders. With age, the activity of the dog's brain reduces and like elderly people they become confused and grumpy, or awkward and slow to accept change. They are often less tolerant of children, who tend to behave in unexpected ways, and where a young dog can accept this, older ones are worried by it and may growl or snap.

The loss of learned behaviour is a commonly noticed change of old age. Old dogs may lose their toilet training. This is usually a sign of fairly advanced senility since toilet training is such a basic part of a dog's upbringing. Most dogs which mess in the house for a reason, such as cystitis, bowel trouble or arthritis which makes it difficult for them to move, will show signs of guilt or distress. When an old dog regularly messes indoors and shows no regret, senility is likely to be the cause.

Geriatric dogs sometimes forget parts of their normal routine. They may look for food at different times of the day, or want to go out in the middle of the night. They may take to lying in unusual places. Aimless behaviour is also a feature of senility. Elderly dogs sometimes take to barking for prolonged periods for no apparent reason. They may wander in a random manner about the house, or follow a set, inexplicable circuit.

It is important to try to adapt to your old dog's changing behaviour. The dog will have limited ability to adapt itself, or learn new routines. In coping with incontinence, for example, try to allow extra opportunities for toileting, and consider moving the dog to a room where the occasional accident will not cause damage and will be easy to clean up. Gently and slowly introduce changes in routine, or new members of the household, human or canine. Try to distract an old dog if he is barking or wandering for no good reason.

As we have mentioned, stimulating the dog's mind may lessen the symptoms of senility. Spending time with him, and encouraging exercise or chewing activity will all help. Providing a younger companion often snaps an old dog out of its lethargy. Companionship, competition and play are all supplied by another dog. The companion, if it is a new dog, should be carefully chosen, though. If your old dog is small or frail, introducing a large, boisterous newcomer is unlikely to be a great success. The right friend, on the other hand, can trigger a second childhood. It often boosts an older dog's self confidence as well, as it will tend to be top dog, at least to start with.

# Summary

- Many character changes in old dogs are secondary to physical disorders

- If you notice a change in behaviour, look for an underlying cause

- Some behaviour changes are simply due to senility

- Young children and old dogs don't always mix

- Be prepared to make allowances and adaptations for your old dog

- Provide plenty of stimulus, and an interesting routine to keep the elderly dog's brain active

- A younger dog may have a rejuvenating effect on an older one – but choose carefully when introducing a new dog

# CHAPTER 4
# Obesity

Obesity is the accumulation of excessive amounts of fat, to the extent that normal bodily function is impaired. It is every bit as important a disorder as those diseases mentioned previously, and elderly dogs are particularly at risk. This is not only because they are more likely to become obese, but also because they are more likely to suffer from the illnesses that obesity may cause or make more severe. Obesity is also a disorder that is rarely taken seriously, perhaps because people are unaware of its dangers or that their pets suffer from the condition at all. And yet, because our dogs are entirely dependent on us for their nutrition, obesity need never occur, and should be simple to cure.

## Why is obesity bad?

Carrying excess amounts of fat adversely affects a dog in many ways. Unfortunately for the elderly dog, many of the diseases of old age are often exacerbated by obesity. In fact, the symptoms of many diseases are only seen because the dog is obese, and returning her body weight to normal will often restore normal function.

Excess fat places extra stress on body systems through the extra work required, in particular by the limbs, skeleton, heart and respiratory system. Imagine a small dog, a Cavalier King Charles Spaniel for instance, 4 or 5 pounds overweight. It doesn't sound much, but this is the equivalent of two bags of sugar strapped to its back. Even a person would soon become weary of carrying that weight around, and one can imagine the extra effort needed by the dog. This also illustrates the value of losing even just a couple of pounds at the start of a diet – the benefit will soon be seen.

Accumulation of fat in and around organs impairs their function. Fat laid down in the liver interferes with the function of liver cells.

Excess fat around the larynx narrows its opening, and causes surrounding tissue such as the soft palate to flop over it, resulting in snoring, shortness of breath and even fainting. Fat around the neck of the bladder and along the urethra may make incontinence more likely. When lying down, the weight and volume of fat in the abdomen of an obese dog can exert enough pressure on the bladder to induce leakage of urine.

Fat is also an extremely good insulator, and fat dogs are at risk of overheating. This is most relevant on a hot summer's day, but a fat dog which overexerts itself at any time is at risk of suffering fatal heat-stroke.

These are some of the major conditions caused by or aggravated by obesity:

- orthopaedic problems (eg arthritis)
- poor exercise tolerance
- congestive heart failure
- breathing difficulties
- reduced liver function
- diabetes mellitus
- poor digestive function (eg constipation or flatulence)
- increased surgical and anaesthetic risk
- reduced resistance to disease
- heat intolerance
- skin disease
- premature or exaggerated ageing
- reduced life expectancy

An additional health risk is caused by the need to treat many of these conditions with drugs, when losing weight may in itself bring about a cure or improvement in symptoms. Many drugs used for arthritis, for example, may aggravate an underlying liver or kidney dysfunction.

# Recognising the obese dog

The obese dog is not hard to recognise, but owners are often the last people to spot the problem. This is usually because obesity comes on slowly, and the dog changes little from day to day. If you have photographs of your pet when he was younger, it may be useful to compare his body condition in years gone by with that of today. Dogs with a thick coat represent a particular problem since they can

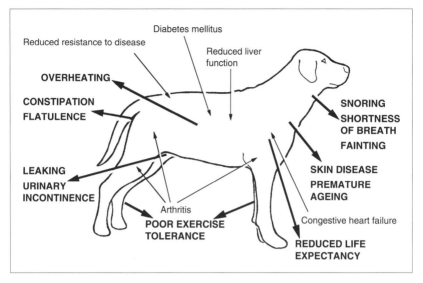

**Figure 4.1** Some problems affecting the obese dog

become quite fat without their owners realising it because their bodies are hidden.

A good guide to your dog's body condition is to feel his ribs. A thin dog, or one in good condition, will have ribs that are easily felt by running a hand along his ribcage. If you have to press to feel the individual ribs, then he is probably overweight, and if you are unable to feel individual ribs at all then he is dangerously overweight.

Some obese dogs may lay down more fat in other places than they do over the ribs so you should check for fat deposits in other areas as well. Under and around the muscle of the lower back and in the abdomen are common sites.

Whenever possible, owners should find a means of weighing their dog. This is useful, partly to identify the problem, and partly to monitor progress once a weight loss program is started. For guidance most veterinary surgeries and books on dog breeds will have a chart of average weights for each breed, although it should be remembered that an individual dog may be towards the lower end of the quoted weight range, but still be obese. All dogs are individuals, and the only way of knowing whether a dog is obese is to go by his body condition.

To weigh a small to medium-sized dog at home, it is best to weigh yourself on the bathroom scales, and then pick him up and weigh yourself again. The difference in the two figures will be his weight. Many veterinary surgeries have scales to weigh dogs on, and this may be the best option for heavier dogs, as the aim is a healthy dog, not an owner with a hernia. Most veterinary surgeons are only too pleased to give advice on whether your dog is overweight, and the control measures required, as curing obesity is part of the general health care service they provide for their patients.

# Reasons for obesity

Apart from a straightforward denial of the fact that a dog is obese, owners of overweight dogs will produce a number of excuses with which most veterinary surgeons are familiar.

### 'Its because he's neutered/she's spayed'
Although it is true that neutered dogs and bitches are more commonly overweight than entire dogs, neutering in itself doesn't cause them to put on more weight.

### 'She only has one meal a day'
This in itself is irrelevant, as one big meal a day is just as capable of making a dog fat as four little ones. It is also often untrue, as further probing reveals that the dog is given a couple of biscuits here, and a choc drop there, and the idea of going without her morning piece of toast is outrageous.

### 'He only has a tiny amount to eat'
This may be true, but it doesn't alter the fact that that tiny amount is still more than is required.

### 'She's old now and can't do much exercise'
This is not an excuse for allowing a dog to become obese. It may also only be true because the dog is obese, and a diet may rejuvenate her.

### 'But he's always hungry'
Dogs have a tremendous ability to look starved even if they are a stone overweight, and dog owners, being the softest touch of all, are always ready to alleviate their obvious suffering. The fact is that dogs are designed to gorge whenever they come across food. In the wild this is a useful trait as the next meal may be 2 or 3 days away. Unfortunately our pet dogs have carried this trait with them into our homes, where the next meal is only as far away as the kitchen cupboard. Don't be suckered by your pet!

The reason for weight gain is simple. A dog has a basic metabolic rate, the tickover at which it uses up energy to keep its body functioning. Any activity will add a certain calorie requirement to this basic rate. The adult dog only needs sufficient calories in its food to cover this basic rate, and any extra activity. If it gets more food than needed to supply these calories, the dog is in *positive energy balance*. If it doesn't receive enough calories to supply the energy used, it is in *negative energy balance*.

In order to be overweight, a dog must have been in positive energy balance for some period of its life without a corresponding period of being in negative energy balance. In other words, if your dog puts on weight at some stage in its life, it is necessary for it to be in negative energy balance for a while in order to return to its normal weight.

There are some factors which make some dogs more likely to put on weight:

- Some breeds, such as Labrador Retrievers, Cocker Spaniels or Dachshunds, seem to be particularly prone.
- Spayed bitches and castrated dogs may have a lower metabolic rate, which may mean that they require 20 to 25 per cent less food after neutering. Don't be misled by this fact into thinking that neutering makes a dog fat. The only way that a dog becomes fat is by receiving more food than it uses.
- Elderly dogs also have a lower metabolic rate – about 20 per cent lower than a young dog.
- Some hormonal conditions, for example hypothyroidism or Cushing's Syndrome, can cause obesity.

# How to cure obesity

There are a couple of principles which are important to grasp before a successful weight control program can be started.

1. No matter how little food a dog appears to be fed, if it is gaining weight, then that amount of food is too much.
2. In order to lose weight (ie use up its fat to provide energy), a dog must be put into negative energy balance (ie starved).

This second point is often missed and needs enlarging upon. Fat has a very low metabolic rate – it doesn't do any work, it just sits there. If we have a Miniature Poodle who weighs 25 pounds, but whose ideal weight should be 15 pounds, this means that there are 10

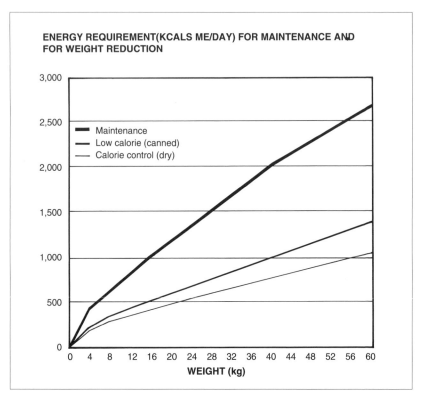

ENERGY REQUIREMENT(KCALS ME/DAY) FOR MAINTENANCE AND FOR WEIGHT REDUCTION

**Figure 4.2** Energy requirements for maintenance and weight reduction

pounds of fat to lose. If we feed him just enough food to cover the metabolic rate for a 25 pound dog, we will be putting him in marked positive energy balance, and he will gain weight.

If we realise the problem, and decide to feed him a maintenance ration for a 15 pound dog, he may not put any more weight on, but because he is receiving all the energy he needs, he won't use up any of the fat, and won't lose any weight.

The correct ration to feed is 60 per cent of the maintenance rate required for his ideal body weight, and he will then start to use some of his fat to provide the shortfall of energy and so lose weight.

Dieting can be carried out successfully using ordinary commercial dog foods, but you may find that you have to feed tiny amounts of food to achieve your aim. There are excellent low calorie prescription diets available from veterinary surgeons in which the calorie content is drastically reduced while still providing enough of the other nutrients and substantial volume. These diets are available in dried and canned forms, and you should be able to find one that is palatable to your dog. If he is initially unwilling to take a low calorie diet, then try mixing the new diet with his normal food in increasing proportions, until you are able to completely change him over. Your veterinary surgeon will also be helpful in advising on a full weight control program.

When we put an obese dog on his diet, the following guidelines will prove helpful:

- **Establish a goal**
  Decide on an ideal weight for the dog (consulting breed standards or a veterinary surgeon). Remember that different individuals within a breed may have differing ideal weights.

- **Decide how much to feed**
  Work out a starting ration as described above – feed 60 per cent of the maintenance requirement for his ideal weight. (Table 4.1 gives the calorie content of some foods. Table 4.2 gives energy allowances for target weights and suggests feeding regimes).

- *Don't* **feed** *any* **titbits or treats**
  One small biscuit or dog treat may not seem like much, but 40 or 50 calories a day will make all the difference between a successful diet and a waste of time. If you really feel unable to avoid giving treats, then take a chunk or two out of his day's food ration and give him that instead. Chunks of carrot are another option, but remember – lots of low calorie treats can still provide as much energy as a single high calorie one. Hide chews will also occupy him, with the added benefit of cleaning his teeth, but they will contain some calories, which must be taken into consideration. One or two a day will be plenty, and they should certainly not be given ad lib.

- **Weigh the dog regularly**
  This is essential, and should be carried out weekly, or fortnightly. Whether you weigh him at home or have him weighed at the veterinary surgeon's, always use the same scales. Keep records of his weight, and make a graph of weight changes. If he fails to lose weight between weighings, reduce his ration by a further 20 per cent each fortnight until he does.

| Food | Energy content K/cals. per 100g |
|---|---|
| Canned dog foods | 75-100 |
| Dog biscuits and meals | 340-390 |
| Complete dry foods | 330-370 |
| Fatty mince | 180-220 |
| Liver | 158-180 |
| Dressed tripe | 70-90 |
| Green tripe | 100 |
| Milk | 65 |
| Bacon | 400-500 |
| Cheese | 300-450 |
| Chocolate | 500 |

**Table 4.1** Energy content of some foods

- **Aim for a gradual weight loss**
  A slow and steady loss of weight and the corresponding increase in fitness is more likely to be long lasting than a dramatic decrease will be. Reasonable rates to expect are:

  | | |
  |---|---|
  | Small dog (eg West Highland) | $^1/_2$ – 1lb/week |
  | Medium dog (eg Springer Spaniel) | 1 – 1$^1/_2$ lb/week |
  | Large dog (eg Labrador) | 1$^1/_2$ - 2$^1/_2$ lb/week |

- **Encourage exercise**
  Exercise helps to burn up calories. It isn't a substitute for dieting, though, and it takes a surprising amount of exercise to burn just a few calories. Too much exercise can be dangerous for the obese dog, so it shouldn't be forced to begin with. As weight is lost, he will become much more lively, and his exercise will be more vigorous, so that his rate of weight loss will improve.

- **Make it easy for the dog**
  His dinner bowl may seem very empty to him when we have worked out the correct ration. Replacing some of the biscuit with a bulky low calorie alternative such as bran or vegetables will make him (and you) feel better. Boiled white or brown rice is a lower calorie alternative to biscuits. Alternatively, use a proprietary obesity diet, which will enable him to eat a greater volume while taking in fewer calories.

| Target weight (kg) | Energy Allowance (K/cals) | Canned slimming diet[1] (g) | Dry slimming diet[2] (g) | Canned + biscuit (g) + (g) |
|---|---|---|---|---|
| less than 3 | up to 150 | up to 150 | up to 45 | up to 75 + up to 25 |
| 3-6 | 150-300 | 150-300 | 45-90 | 75-150 + 25-50 |
| 6-10 | 300-450 | 300-450 | 90-135 | 150-225 + 50-75 |
| 10-15 | 450-600 | 450-600 | 135-180 | 225-300 + 75-100 |
| 15-20 | 600-750 | 600-750 | 180-230 | 300-375 + 100-125 |
| 20-25 | 750-900 | 750-900 | 230-270 | 375-450 + 125-150 |
| 25-30 | 900-1000 | 900-1000 | 270-300 | 450-500 +150-170 |
| 30-35 | 1000-1150 | 1000-1150 | 300-350 | 500-575 + 170-190 |
| 35-40 | 1150-1250 | 1150-1250 | 350-380 | 575-625 + 190-210 |
| 40-45 | 1250-1350 | 1250-1350 | 380-410 | 625-675 + 210-225 |
| 45-50 | 1350-1500 | 1350-1500 | 410-450 | 675-750 + 225-250 |
| 50-60 | 1500-1700 | 1500-1700 | 450-515 | 750-850 + 250-285 |
| 60-70 | 1700-1900 | 1700-1900 | 515-575 | 850-950 +285-320 |
| 70+ | 1900+ | 1900+ | 575+ | 950+ 320+ |

1 For example Pedigree Canine Low Calorie Diet (Waltham)
2 For example Doggy lo-calorie (Leo Laboratories)

**Table 4.2** Suggested feeding regime for obese dogs

- **Get family and friends on the team**
  If you think that uncles, aunts and grandparents spoil your children, wait until you see what they do to your dog. Many a diet is torpedoed because the less food you give him, the more biscuits the neighbours drop over the fence. Ensure that everyone who has contact with the dog understands that their kindness is killing him, and the diet is a positive and necessary step back to good health.

Once you have followed these guidelines for a few weeks, you may congratulate yourself on having a new dog – fit, active, healthy and happy.

# Prevention of obesity

As about 50 per cent of us come to realise at Christmas, a week of excess can take 11 months of self-sacrifice to rectify. In other words, prevention is not only better than a cure, it is a lot easier. Follow some simple rules to ensure your dog remains slim.

1) Some breeds are more liable to become obese. Examples are Labrador Retrievers, Dachshunds, Cocker Spaniels and Collies. If your dog is a member of one of these breeds, be aware that you may only need to feed them a small ration, and that they are likely to put on weight if given any titbits
2) Neutering does reduce a dog's energy requirement. After your bitch is spayed, or your dog castrated, monitor its weight carefully, and be prepared to reduce its ration by up to 25 per cent of its normal amount
3) Ageing also reduces a dog's energy requirement by about 20 per cent. Reduce the calories fed as your dog ages.
4) Try not to get into the habit of feeding titbits. Once a dog is used to them, you will find that it is hard to break *yourself* of the habit. Don't fool yourself that you can't refuse him – if you don't give him one, he'll do without
5) Weigh your dog regularly. By noticing any increase in weight at an early stage, you will make it easy to correct.
6) Don't kid yourself – a fat dog isn't a happy one. A moment's joy at receiving a treat it probably doesn't even taste can't make up for the lethargy, the pain of arthritis or the breathlessness of heart failure and respiratory disease that may result from obesity.

# Summary

- Obesity is a serious disorder, and one that elderly dogs are especially at risk from

- There is only one real reason for obesity – we are feeding the affected dog more than it requires

- Dieting is not cruel – at the least it will prolong a dog's life, at best it will rejuvenate him and relieve much suffering

- Prevention is far easier than cure – be aware of the ageing dog's falling energy requirements and adapt its diet accordingly

# The Ageing Dog

# CHAPTER 5
# The home environment

As your dog ages, the home which it has known for so long and generally takes for granted appears to change in character. In many ways it presents a very different and more problematical environment to the older dog than it did when it was young. We should try to recognise these difficulties and do what we can to ease their life and so help them cope. We should also realise that old dogs may need some luxuries and concessions if they are to remain happy and content.

## Hazards in the home and garden

Many of the difficulties that the older dog experiences in the home will be directly related to its reduced mobility and agility although failing eyesight and general senility also contribute to the problem. The following are some of the obstacles and situations which may cause difficulties from time to time.

### Stairs and steps
With gradually stiffening limbs, old dogs find it increasingly painful to go up and down stairs. What was easy in their earlier life may become quite hazardous as they become less agile. They become more likely to lose their footing and fall as a result. This becomes even more likely if their eyesight is poor. The action of climbing stairs puts strain on their back and may bring on or aggravate troubles such as 'slipped' discs and pulled muscles. Even the smallest flight of steps around the home and garden may prove difficult to negotiate.

It is obviously best to remove the need to go up and down stairs, for example, by having the dog's bed downstairs. A dog used to sleeping upstairs at night may be unwilling to change the habit of a lifetime .

You may need to be firm and it may be necessary to use a stairgate to enforce your will. Ensure his new bed is warm and comfortable (see below), and perhaps give him a chew or treat in the bed to encourage him to stay there. If it is unavoidable that he needs to go upstairs, try to minimise the number of steps that the dog has to cope with and, if possible, always be there to help him up and down.

## Slippery floors

Floors that are not carpeted are often disliked by older dogs. Stiff limbs, hard slippery pads and long nails all contribute to a feeling of insecurity. Slipping on such flooring often leads to injury of the ageing limbs so, if possible, the need to walk on them should be eliminated. If your ageing dog has to cross such floors, an old rug or something similar to cover it up may be advisable even if you do lift it when guests visit! The geriatric should definitely not be shut in a room where there is no flooring which offers a good grip.

## Changes in furniture

Moving furniture around, or altering the house in other ways can confuse elderly dogs. Often a dog with bad eyesight will have memorised the positions of major obstacles in the home and does not consciously visualise them every time he comes across them. If you do need to change things around, stay with the dog for a while to allow him time to familiarise himself with the new layout.

## Fires and heaters

Old dogs will tend to seek out warm places to sleep and rest. They have the capacity for deep sleep from which they find it hard to rouse themselves. It is possible that they may lie near or up against a source of excessive heat and, as a result, suffer burns before they are aware of it. It may be necessary to treat them like young children and place a fireguard around fires and other heat sources.

## Garden ponds

Poor eyesight and tottery limbs make ageing dogs likely candidates to fall into garden ponds and swimming pools. If they are unlucky enough to fall in, they may not be strong or agile enough to get out, or to swim for long and drowning is a very real danger. Even if it is only a shallow pond from which they can escape easily, they may injure themselves in the process or become chilled. Some robust form of fencing may be necessary, or if this is not possible, you may need to isolate the dog from the part of the garden presenting the hazard.

### People

An elderly dog which is asleep or which has poor hearing can be oblivious to its surroundings, including approaching people. They are frequently trodden on or kicked by mistake, and may be as much a danger to the person involved as to themselves. Try to encourage them to sleep in their own beds, or at least be vigilant and be prepared for them to be lying in the most awkward of places.

# Bedding

Old dogs will spend a large proportion of their time asleep, and it will be more convenient for you, and more comfortable for them if you can get them to do this in a bed of their own.

From the dog's point of view, a bed and bedding should be warm, comfortable and dry. Older dogs may be incontinent, usually with urine and sometimes with faeces, either because they find it difficult to get up and go outside to toilet or sometimes because they are just too deeply asleep to stop themselves. From your point of view, therefore, desirable points are easy cleaning, low odour and durability.

Because of the amount of time spent lying down and their thinning and less elastic skin, ageing dogs are prone to calluses on their elbows and hocks. These are, at best, unsightly, and at worst they can crack, become infected and sore and so are best avoided. The correct bedding should prevent them occurring but if they do, daily application of petroleum jelly will often prevent these complications.

Finally, old dogs are often, unfortunately, by nature a little smelly and bedding material will need to be easily and frequently cleaned.

## Bedding design

A bed with a raised edge is best, as it will protect the dog from draughts, and be generally warmer. Wicker or fabric beds are available, but if there is any chance of accidents, a plastic bed will protect the carpet. A cotton sheet or several layers of newspaper can be used as the lining to the bed and this will provide insulation, and help mop up any leaks.

For the dog to lie on, I would strongly recommend fleecy bedding material, often known as veterinary bedding. This consists of a polyester fur fabric on a strong porous backing. These beds are very warm and their thick pile will help to avoid the formation of calluses. They allow fluid to pass through them, whilst the top remains dry, so that incontinent dogs will not be lying in wet beds. They are hygienic and easy to clean being machine washable and even after years of daily washing, they are still comfortable, warm and effective. These types of beds are available through veterinary surgeries, pet shops and direct from the suppliers through newspaper and magazine advertising.

Some other types of bedding are worth considering, especially if incontinence and soiling is not a problem. Bean bags conform to the shape of the dog as it lies down so that they support the whole body firmly and evenly. The polystyrene beads which fill these beds are excellent insulators and are, therefore, very warm. Their outer cover needs to be washable, and the inner cover should be as tough as possible to avoid tearing when stood on.

A recent development is bedding consisting of aluminium foil strips contained in a small quilt-like cover. Various outer covers can be used, including cotton and waterproof materials. The aluminium foil is a very good insulating medium and so reflects back the heat of the dog, making these beds very warm for old dogs prone to chilling.

All parts of the bedding should be washed frequently to ensure good hygiene, to reduce  odour build up and prevent flea eggs collecting.

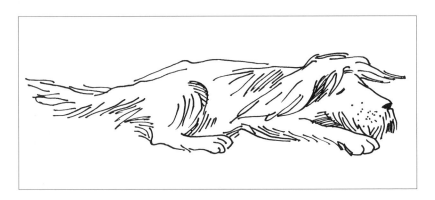

# Concessions to old age

As your dog ages it will prove necessary to change his daily routine in several ways, both for his benefit and for yours. You cannot expect to treat the old dog in the same way as he has been treated throughout his younger life, otherwise accidents, discomfort and ill health will result.

Some of the changes relate to the dangers that the home presents to the geriatric, and we have mentioned these above. Some of the other alterations in routine include:

# Changing the sleeping place

Elderly dogs are less well able to maintain their body temperature because of falling metabolic rate, thinning of the coat and loss of weight so it may be necessary to move the bed even if they are already sleeping downstairs. If they have been accustomed to sleeping in a cool room, or outside in a kennel or garage, you may have to consider bringing them in to a warmer room. Alternatively you may need to provide some form of heating, such as an infra-red lamp or heated pads. Allowing the dog to get cold will put stress on all the body systems particularly the joints and muscles so causing lameness and stiffness.

Many elderly dogs become incontinent because they have reduced bladder capacity and control and, as a result, sometimes leak a little urine where they lie down. They may also lose some bowel control and soil indoors on occasions. Declining skin and coat quality may mean that the skin itself may contribute to the odour many older dogs possess. This overall body odour may mean that it is better to place a dog's sleeping quarters in a room away from the living part of the house. It may also be better to use a room in which the floor is not carpeted such as a kitchen or utility room. A dog may act as if it is rejected when first moved, but this seldom lasts especially if a comfortable bed is provided.

# Changing toilet habits

As we have mentioned, old dogs are likely to have reduced bladder capacity and bladder and bowel control. We must appreciate this and be sympathetic if accidents occur. Often the dog is itself upset by messing indoors, which goes against deeply ingrained training. Displaying anger will simply increase the dog's stress levels and the anxiety caused makes future accidents more likely.

Instead we need to provide more opportunity for our dog to relieve itself. This means allowing her out as early as possible in the morning and as late as possible at night, and more often in between times. Don't hurry her, as reduced muscle tone in bladder and bowel may mean that more than one attempt is required to empty out. Old dogs may be reluctant to go out simply because it's cold or because their limbs are aching. Try to encourage them out, and ensure that painful conditions such as arthritis receive treatment. Many elderly dogs which apparently develop incontinence undergo a miraculous cure once their joint disease is treated.

Some degree of diet control will help with bowel control. Avoiding large meals in the evening will lessen the strain on the digestive system, and avoiding rich foods will reduce the chances of diarrhoea occurring. Water should always be freely available and particularly for the old dog, so withholding water is not an option for coping with urinary incontinence except under veterinary advice.

## Changing feeding habits

Through reduced appetite and impaired efficiency of the digestive system, elderly dogs may find it hard to cope with a single large meal a day and as a result may not finish their meal at one sitting. Even if they do, they may not be able to digest it properly, giving rise to digestive upsets such as diarrhoea and flatulence and inadequate nutrition.

It is best to split the daily ration into several meals. Initially 2 meals a day will probably be enough, but as a dog becomes older and more frail, as many as 4 meals a day may be better. Although this may seem inconvenient, as long as your dog is basically healthy and doesn't need a special diet, then a good quality dried food can be used. This is usually more convenient than canned or home-cooked food and considerably cheaper. See Chapter 8 for more on nutrition of the older dog.

## Tolerance of senility

The very elderly dog will often show signs of senility. She may demand more attention from you and want to be close to you as much as possible. She may bark at nothing, ignore you when you speak to her, be intolerant of change and stubborn. Try to be understanding. Give as much time to her as you can spare, be sure to have plenty of physical contact with her and talk to her frequently. All these tokens of affection will be much appreciated by old dogs, keeping them content and secure. Punishment, be it verbal, physical or by depriving her of your company, may have a very stressful effect on an elderly dog and this will contribute to a decline in her general health and happiness.

# Leaving the aged dog

It may become difficult to leave an elderly dog for short or long periods of time although some will simply sleep and be quite content if left for long periods. Others, however, may become distressed and worried. Their reduced bladder and bowel control must be considered, not just because of the mess they leave you to clean up, but also because of the upset it may cause them. Try to ensure that the older dog isn't left alone for more than a few hours at a time. Perhaps they can be looked after by a neighbour or relative for short periods during the day if all members of the household are at work. Some elderly dogs will need feeding several times during the day, and these meals need to be spaced out. It is of little use to feed 4 meals a day if they are given at 7am and 6, 8 and 10pm to fit in with the household's daily routine.

Going away for holidays may present problems as well. Leaving the old dog in kennels may be upsetting for her if she has never been left before. She may not receive the comforts or company she requires and may be disorientated and distressed. This stress may aggravate or induce a variety of disease conditions. Her resistance to disease is also likely to be low thus making her more susceptible to diseases to which she may be exposed in the kennels.

Ideally you will be able to leave her at home with someone living in the house. In this way she will be in her own familiar environment even if it is a stranger looking after her. Alternatively you may be able to take her with you, or maybe your kind neighbour/relative who should be aware of her daily needs would be prepared to look after her in a nearby home for a week or two.

There is often no easy answer to the care of the older dog but these factors mentioned must be considered, confirming that the geriatric dog can often be a considerable tie.

# Younger dogs

Bringing a new dog into the home can be a mixed blessing as far as the older dog is concerned. In many cases having a younger dog around gives the older one a new lease of life with geriatrics previously showing signs of senility becoming livelier and more alert. They are keener to exercise, trying to keep up with the young animal, and frequently eat better through the stimulation of this exercise or the need to ensure that the incomer doesn't get their share as well. The company provided by a younger dog is often comforting and may overcome some of the problems of leaving an elderly dog unattended.

On the other hand, older dogs can be intolerant of young animals. They may be irritated by their liveliness and constant desire to play. This may lead them to be snappy with the new dog, and as the new one grows in confidence fights may ensue. They will usually settle down eventually, but care must be taken to ensure that the old dog is not injured before this occurs. The young dogs may bully old ones, particularly at mealtimes so it may be better to feed the dogs in separate rooms or at separate times if necessary.

On balance a young companion is usually more a blessing than a trial to the elderly dog, but it is important to consider beforehand the type of dog to be introduced, and the age of the existing resident. Although maybe an extreme example, introducing a boisterous, large Labrador puppy when you already have a 13 year old Yorkshire Terrier is unlikely to be the best of ideas. Try to bring the new dog into the household while the older dog is still relatively healthy and able to stand up for itself. Very old dogs are more likely than 'young' geriatrics to have their noses put out of joint by new arrivals.

## Young children

The arrival of a new young human being is less likely to be welcomed by the venerable old dog. Humans often get a dog when they are young and single, and the dog is their best companion. By the time the person has been married for some time and then had a child, their dog is likely to be mature, and may be approaching old age. Although it is natural for a new child to take up all of its parents' attention, they should try not to neglect the dog too much. This is important for all dogs so that they don't view the child as too much of a rival, but is especially so for older dogs.

If there are older children in the house or the dog has not had much contact with children, he may be more grumpy and liable to snap if disturbed. This is usually because they don't like the noise and rapid movement of children and this may be made more significant if they have poor eyesight and hearing. It is important to instil a sense of respect for the dog into your own children, and teach them that he shouldn't be teased or disturbed. Try to ensure that children don't creep up on aged dogs, particularly when resting or sleeping, but rather make the dog aware that they are approaching by talking to it. When children visit you, it may be best to shut the geriatric dog away for everyone's protection, and the least strain all round. You may identify with your dog's desire to bite an unruly child, but it may spoil your relationship with the parents.

# Summary

- As your dog ages, the home it is used to can become a bit of an obstacle course. Stairs, slippery floors and fires are some of the hazards

- Well chosen bedding will improve your dog's comfort and health, and prevent soiling of your house while being easy to clean.

- Aged dogs are more demanding and inflexible. You may have to make concessions and alterations to your own routine as well as the dog's.

- Younger dogs can be rejuvenating for geriatrics, but the wrong choice of a young companion can cause upset and stress.

- Old dogs and children are not always the best combination. Always be aware of the safety of children and the feelings of your dog.

# CHAPTER 6
# Exercise and activity

The requirement and capacity for exercise in the older dog will be markedly different from that of the young adult. Reduced willingness and reduced capability must be taken into account. We must accept that our dog may be feeling the effects of old age, even if in our mind's eye, he is still a dog in his prime, able to run all day and still be asking to play ball when he gets home. Exercise is necessary, however, and the trick is to know the dog's limitations and allow him to satisfy his wish for exercise within these.

## Is exercise important?

It is an easy thing, as we watch our ageing pet sleeping comfortably by a radiator, or wince as he stiffly uncurls from his basket, to convince ourselves that the old fellow doesn't need or want to go out for a walk. This is a particularly attractive theory if we are busy, or the nights are long and cold, and a walk in the cold, damp park doesn't really appeal to the human half of the partnership. There are many reasons why exercise is beneficial, however, and we should try to ensure that he has at least a little. One of the major benefits of dogs as companions is that they force us to get out and about every day, and I'm sure that many dogs see our usefulness as fitness consultants as one of our two main plus points (the other being our ability to provide food).

### Interest

Just as we ourselves do, dogs will become stale minded if they are confined to the house and garden. They may not appear to mind, or perhaps may even seem reluctant to come out when invited, but the lack of different experiences will surely contribute to speedier ageing of their minds. Many dogs put exercise as their number one priority, even before food. This is not just because they are fitness freaks – many a Spaniel is keen as mustard to get out on a walk, then will infuriate its owner by pottering around the first fence post it comes to for an eternity. The main attraction is interest. For a species of animal designed to be on the move all the day long, forced confinement can cause unhappiness and mental disturbance. Dogs are also highly social, and although they are faithful to us and accept the human family as a reasonable surrogate pack, we can't provide the fantastic smells and experiences that the two bitches up the road can. Allowing the elderly dog to be in a different environment a few times daily will keep it alert, and give him something to look forward to. Even if he goes to the same places each day for his exercise, this will break up the monotony of the day and allow him to keep up with events in the neighbourhood.

## Fitness

Daily exercise is important to keep the muscles working effectively and keep them healthy. Muscle tissue needs to be stimulated to retain its bulk and vigour. If we are unfortunate enough to suffer an injury which puts one limb out of action we will soon notice the wasting of the muscles. Even two weeks inactivity will make a marked difference. When the time comes to start using the limb again, the muscles will be weak, necessitating much physiotherapy and exercise to restore normal muscle bulk and tone. In the same way, if a dog spends all its time lying about inactive, its muscle tissue will waste, leaving it weak so that it is less inclined to exercise. Even if you can persuade him to go for a walk, weak muscles won't give sufficient support to the joints, making injuries more likely, and worsening the effects of chronic disease such as arthritis.

It is as true for a dog as for a person that *mens sana in corpore sano*, a healthy mind resides in a healthy body. Once a dog becomes inactive and unfit, stagnation of the mind will follow, and the onset of senility will be hastened.

## Obesity

As we have already mentioned, the basic metabolic rate of geriatric dogs may fall by up to 20 per cent. Lack of exercise will further reduce the energy usage of the dog (see Chapter 4). Regular exercise is important as an aid to keeping weight down, and almost essential in any weight loss program. Once an elderly dog has become fat and inactive, it will lose much of its ability to exercise, and some dogs may never be able to return to their former level of fitness.

# Appetite

Some elderly dogs have a reduced appetite, rather than an obesity problem. Gentle exercise is helpful in stimulating appetite. If weight loss is a problem, it should be possible to provide more calories than are used at exercise in the extra food eaten as a result of that stimulation.

# Bowels

Bowel disorders are common problems of old age. Constipation in particular may be suffered. Getting a dog out and about on two or more occasions a day will stimulate regular bowel movements, and discourage the retention that can occur through inactivity. Giving plenty of opportunity for voiding the bowels may also help with the problem of lack of faecal control in the home.

# Heart/lungs

Regular exercise helps to keep the heart and respiratory muscles well toned. Naturally this can be overdone in old and frail dogs, but under-exercising is far more frequent than over-exercising. Dogs with congestive heart failure suffer from fluid collecting in lung tissue, and sometimes in the limbs causing swollen legs. If capable of gentle exercise, the pumping action of respiratory and locomotor muscles working will help to clear much of this fluid.

# Arthritis

Dogs suffering from arthritis will be much stiffer and have more painful joints when at rest than when they are moving about. Gentle activity and warming of the joints improves comfort, and an arthritic dog should be encouraged to take steady exercise. Too little exercise reduces the range of movement that the joints are capable of. Movement breaks down fibrosis and scar tissue. Extended or vigorous exercise will bring worse stiffness the next day however, and is to be avoided.

# How much exercise is needed?

The quantity of exercise given to the ageing dog should be carefully matched to his capabilities and state of health. There is no typical aged dog. They range from 'Can't sit still Collies' and 'Tearaway Terriers' to 'Leave me alone Labradors' and 'Creaky Cairns'. Many

elderly dogs will have a great capacity for exercise and keep up well with younger canine additions to the family. This is fine as long as you are sure that they are up to it. Dogs aren't always sensible however, and apart from the risks to their health of ten mile runs, they are not always the only ones to suffer. It isn't always very amusing when Boris the Basset decides that the two miles across the moors from the car were great, but now he's pooped and you will have to carry him back, complete with some very interesting fox scent he found to roll in on the way.

For the majority of elderly dogs the watchword is steady. As they age, however young at heart they feel, or you fondly imagine them to be, their body will tend to let them down from time to time. Less flexible joints and weaker muscles make strains and sprains more common, and they will recover more slowly. Dogs in the early stages of arthritis may be willing to run for miles, but they will pay for it after resting, and may spend the whole of the next day stiff and uncomfortable.

For most elderly dogs regular steady exercise is much preferable to occasional long walks. The distance walked is not critical, but most old dogs should be taken out for at least 20 minutes twice daily. Longer than this is fine, as long as it isn't forced, and you don't see signs of excessive stiffness afterwards. Be guided by your dog. You shouldn't have to force him to walk for that length of time. If you do, he may not be capable of it. The walking needn't be vigorous. If an elderly dog only potters about sniffing various scents during his exercise, he will still be getting benefit from it.

Dogs with severe arthritis or advanced heart or respiratory disease may not be capable of doing much exercise. Unless under orders to rest, even these dogs can benefit from getting out and gently walking.

If they are incapable of moving far, they will appreciate being taken out, even if just to the end of the garden to sniff the air and feel the sun.

It is easy to assume that because a dog is getting old there is no need to give it more exercise than it can get from walking in the garden, but you and the dog will feel the better for it if you can get outside and stretch your legs properly.

# What sort of exercise?

As we have said, the exercise given to elderly dogs should be steady. This needn't mean sedate, but forced marches and accompanying jogging owners are not to be encouraged. The exercise given to older dogs should be designed to bring about the benefits mentioned above, whilst avoiding injury and overexertion.

The twisting and turning involved in playing football or chasing bouncing balls is particularly liable to cause joint injuries. These can become chronic, or lead to arthritis in the affected joints. This type of exercise is to be avoided as far as possible. If your dog enjoys chasing and fetching, try to throw a softer ball, or a throw toy such as a ring, which will do less bouncing. This activity should be restricted to short bursts, compromising between the enjoyment gained by the dog and the potential damage she may suffer. Throwing of sticks, incidentally, is not recommended for dogs of any age, as stick injuries to the back of the mouth and throat are common and often serious.

Similarly, chasing and playing with younger dogs can lead to injuries. Much enjoyment is gained from this activity, so I would be loath to stop older dogs from taking part in it, but they should be restrained if the chase is too hectic, and they should be limited to a few minutes at a time of this type of play.

The dog should be discouraged from too much jumping, especially from high places, as this again will result in injury.

If your dog is capable of it, then normal walking and running are fine. Activities such as agility training can still be enjoyed, but may need to be modified. For many older dogs the jumping and twisting incurred in this form of exercise may be too much. If your dog has a heart or respiratory condition, or suffers severe arthritis, the exercise given will have to be gentle and probably short. Several short walks a day will not tax most elderly dogs and will still provide much benefit.

Swimming is an activity that many dogs enjoy and is excellent exercise particularly if they suffer from arthritis or joint conditions.

Stiff old dogs will often find it easier to exercise in water than out because of the support given to their bodies. As they age, however, you should try to limit swimming to only when the weather is warm and the dog can be dried immediately afterwards. The chilling effect of damp skin and coat after swimming may aggravate the discomfort of arthritis and muscular pains and undo any good which might have been done by the exercise. Damp and cold may also affect an elderly dog's chest, perhaps causing a flare up of bronchitis or, even worse, pneumonia. Remember though, swimming is hard work, and frail dogs and those affected by heart and respiratory disorders may be at risk of exhaustion or cardiac arrest if they overdo the swimming.

# Precautions

If your dog suffers from a disorder which limit its ability to exercise such as heart or respiratory disease, or arthritis, then plan his exercise carefully. You should be thinking of short walks, perhaps several times a day making sure that you do not stray far from home or the car. If he collapses, or is unable to walk after a while you are going to have to get him back, which may mean carrying him or supporting his rear legs. If he is too big for you to manage on your own, you may need to ensure that you have a friend who can come with you, or exercise him in a place where other people are available to help.

Elderly dogs often suffer poor hearing and/or sight. This must be taken into consideration when walking them. They can be a danger to themselves and traffic near roads. If they stray out of sight they may lose and be unable to locate you, so that you have to be sure of their whereabouts at all times.

Dogs which are becoming senile will sometimes have a tendency to wander aimlessly. In the home this is not a great problem, but when outdoors it may be disastrous. They can become confused and follow anyone who happens to walk by. At best it can be embarrassing to have to explain that you weren't trying to palm off your aged dog while you went looking for a new model; at worst your dog may be led off in totally the wrong direction and be comprehensively lost.

Old dogs' reactions to other dogs at exercise vary greatly. They may be nervous of younger, more lively dogs, especially if they are not very mobile themselves. Some ageing dogs can be aggressive towards younger ones, perhaps because they feel threatened by their liveliness, and they are frustrated by their inability to keep up or escape. Whether they are aggressive or nervous the older dog should be kept on the lead and close to you if young dogs approach. Many elderly dogs are of course quite happy to see and walk with young ones.

Aged dogs are at risk of drowning when exercised near rivers, canals or ponds. They are likely to stumble into water because of poor eyesight and unsteady legs, and once in the water may not be strong enough to get out or remain afloat for long. Particular care must be taken if you take your dog to such places.

For several of the reasons above, it is worth considering using an extending lead when exercising the older dog, to retain better control.

# Summary

---

- Exercise is beneficial in several ways to the ageing dog – it provides interest, keeps them fit, helps appetite and bowel function, and keeps stiff joints mobile

- Be sure that your dog is capable of taking exercise – your vet will advise on this

- Always exercise your dog within its capabilities – several short walks a day are more beneficial than one long one

- Avoid extended periods of vigorous exercise, jumping, twisting and turning, which can lead to exhaustion or injuries

- Remember that you will have to get your dog home if he decides that he can't walk any further

- Remember that old dogs need to be watched carefully at exercise – they are at risk of injury or getting lost, particularly if blind, deaf or senile

---

# CHAPTER 7
# General care

All dogs require a certain amount of attention during life if they are to remain healthy and happy. As they age, however, it becomes more important to give them this attention, and inevitably they will need more care if the quality of their life is to be maintained. Good observation on behalf of the owner is important so that any changes in their pet's health will be noticed early. Increasing patience and tolerance from the whole family will also be necessary as an older dog's house manners fall into decline. To add insult to injury, the ageing dog often doesn't appreciate the extra care needed, and becomes inflexible and irritable.

It is a fortunate dog that doesn't develop one or more of the diseases of old age during the latter years of life. As has been discussed earlier, many diseases can be treated or alleviated, and the earlier that treatment is started, the more the benefit. Get into the habit of noticing how your dog behaves, what its appetite is like for example, its toileting behaviour, its coat condition. Daily grooming gives a good opportunity to observe any symptoms of disorder. See Appendix 1 for a complete health check list for the ageing dog.

# Grooming

Grooming, which is not just brushing and combing the coat, but attention to the whole dog, should be carried out at least daily when a dog becomes elderly. Of several benefits, the following are especially important:

- Ensures contact between you and your dog. This is appreciated more than you may imagine, especially if your dog is blind, deaf or unable to exercise much.
- Allows you to examine the dog for signs of ill health.
- Keeps your dog looking at her best, and reduces the soiling and odours which are unfortunately part of old age.
- Can help to prevent some disorders of old age from occurring.

For your comfort and convenience, it is usually best to carry out grooming with your dog on a table covered with some form of waterproof and non-slip cover such as a rubber sheet. If your dog has been used to grooming throughout its life, then the more frequent attention needed in older life shouldn't worry her. Some dogs are unfortunately unwilling to put up with this attention at any stage and this may be especially true of dogs as they age if their temper becomes shorter. Try to make grooming time pleasurable for your dog. Some will enjoy the attention anyway but others may need persuading. Talk to them as you examine them. Be gentle (if possible). For the purposes of persuasion a treat may be given after you have finished, but don't overdo this. Apart from the need to avoid weight gain, dogs quickly learn if awkward behaviour results in a treat being given, and will play up all the more. Whoever coined the phrase about not being able to teach an old dog new tricks may have been technically correct, but nothing says that they can't learn them themselves!

## The practicalities
Although in general dogs shouldn't be bathed too often, bathing may be necessary from time to time. Aged dogs often need bathing more

frequently usually because their skins and coats tend to be more greasy and smelly often predisposing them to skin disease. Whilst most dogs will only need bathing every one to six months, those affected with some skin diseases will benefit from more frequent bathing with medicated shampoos, sometimes as often as every day. Persistent parasite infestations are another reason for more frequent bathing, particularly during the summer months.

As long as it isn't too distressing for the dog, bathing of geriatrics is quite acceptable. It is important to remember that the water should be pleasant to the dog (lukewarm) and that they should be well dried afterwards, and have somewhere warm and draught free to lie when bath time is over. Special mild shampoos which are less likely to harm the skin should be used whenever possible. Dry shampoos which are massaged into the coat and then brushed out may be useful for particularly frail dogs. See Appendix 2 for a check list for grooming and cleaning the elderly dog.

# Dental care

Dental disease is extremely common amongst ageing dogs, and its effects can range from bad breath to extreme pain and can give rise to other apparently unrelated diseases such as loss of appetite, pneumonia and heart infections.

Dental problems begin as plaque on the teeth which soon becomes calcified to form tartar. The bacteria which form plaque can cause infection in and inflammation of the gums, which is called gingivitis. The build up of tartar pushing between the teeth damages the gums and allows infection to become established eventually eroding the gums and bone of the teeth sockets. Pus gathers in the pockets formed by this erosion, is swallowed, infecting the throat and stomach, and enters the bloodstream to be carried to heart, lungs and other organs.

Many owners are unaware that their dog has a problem with his teeth, as they usually don't see much of the dog's mouth. Even when they do see his teeth, it is usually the small incisors and large canines at the front of the mouth, and these form only a small part of the total mouth space. In addition, it is usually the large upper premolars and molars that are the teeth which first become dirty. Make a point of lifting up your dogs lip and examining the teeth at the back of the mouth as well as the front. Many of you will be surprised at what you find. The signs of dental disease are halitosis, brown tartar on the teeth, and red or bleeding gums. There may be pus leaking from some sockets and loose teeth. The dog may show discomfort when the teeth are examined and have some difficulty eating.

## Prevention

We can, using a few simple techniques, significantly slow down or prevent completely the development of dental disease. If tartar is already present, it is important that a proper dental scaling is first carried out by your veterinary surgeon. Having scaled the teeth, your vet will polish them to repair the damage done to the surface of the enamel by the build up of tartar and by the scaling process. This will leave a smooth surface so slowing the rate of new tartar build up.

If your dog is fortunate enough to have clean teeth already, you should still clean the teeth daily. Although initially this may seem excessive, we wouldn't dream of cleaning our own teeth less often and contrary to what many believe, dogs have no magic self-cleaning system of their own. If we only brushed our teeth once a week we would soon feel the discomfort of gingivitis and experience a build up of tartar. Our breath wouldn't be all that attractive either. Having said that, any level of cleaning is better than none at all. Once your dog is used to the cleaning process, it need not take long, nor be much of a chore.

It is best to use a toothpaste specifically designed for dogs. Human toothpaste is not designed to be swallowed. It contains foaming agents which your dog will find unpleasant. Doggy toothpaste is usually flavoured attractively in malt, beef, chicken etc. and is safe to swallow in reasonable quantities. The best type to use is available from veterinary surgeons and contains an enzyme system which becomes activated on contact with saliva, releasing chemicals which destroy bacteria. If gingivitis has started already, a tooth gel containing chlorhexidine is an effective oral antiseptic and may provide some relief. Abrasive pastes are also available which can be used if small amounts of tartar are present and a full scaling is not required. These should not be used too often, as they will wear away enamel. The dog has a much thinner layer of enamel on its teeth than we do, and as enamel is not formed after the adult teeth have developed, once lost it will not be replaced.

A soft bristled brush may be used to clean the teeth. Those designed specifically for dogs are available from your veterinary surgery, or you can use a child's toothbrush or a soft cloth. Finger brushes, soft rubber tubes which fit over a finger and have soft rubber bristles attached, are particularly convenient to use. Brush the outer surfaces of all the teeth with a gentle circular motion, paying particular attention to the border between gum and tooth. It is not so important to clean the inner surfaces as these usually only become affected after the outer surfaces. If the gums bleed a little after brushing, this is a sign that they are inflamed but you should persevere, and they will soon be healthier and tougher. If brushing really does prove impossible, then oral sprays and mouthwashes containing chlorhexidine are available as a compromise.

If your dog is unused to having his teeth cleaned or examined, then start off by getting him used to it by placing some of the toothpaste on your finger and allowing him to lick it off. Then rub your finger on his teeth and gums and lift his lips to allow examination of and access to the back teeth. It is particularly important to ensure that these are cleaned properly.

There are several dental aids available, many of which are enjoyable for the dog. Hide chews are useful and when new may help to crack lumps of tartar off the teeth. As the dog chews them and they soften, they make excellent toothbrushes, rubbing the tooth surfaces and massaging the gums. Some chews are impregnated with the same enzymes found in veterinary toothpastes. Although bones are good for cleaning teeth, they are not recommended as they may fracture teeth or cause problems if swallowed.

Rubber toys with grooves to apply toothpaste are also available. There is even an oral gel which delivers active incredients to the teeth and gums and remains in contact long enough to work without requiring brushing. If you can, however, physical brushing with a suitable toothpaste is still the best method of maintaining dental hygiene.

# Avoiding stress

Stress is a term which covers both physical and mental insult and because of their declining physical and mental health, aged dogs are likely to be much more susceptible to it than young dogs. Either form of stress should be avoided as it will have an adverse effect on the elderly dog, reducing her resistance to infections and other disease and making her generally unhappy. Disease processes which might not ordinarily cause problems may blow up to become serious. If you succeed in avoiding stress in your ageing dog by feeding well, exercising sensibly, giving her a warm and comfortable sleeping area, getting treatment for diseases or painful disorders and ensuring that she is happy and secure, then you will be carrying out most of what is necessary to have a happy and healthy elderly dog.

The following are factors that may cause stress:

- Becoming cold, especially for long periods.
- Exhaustion at exercise.
- Unwelcome disturbance, if there is no escape for the old dog, eg children, young dogs.
- Fright, eg fireworks, children, unfamiliar surroundings.
- Being apart from owners and the home, eg kennels, travel.
- Poor diet, deficient in any of the necessary nutrients, or too rich in the wrong nutrients.
- Obesity.
- Pain, eg arthritis, dental disease, tumours.
- Untreated diseases, such as heart, kidney, liver and dental disease.

# Travelling and holidays

There will be times when you will want to take your elderly dog on journeys or on holiday with you. If used to travelling, and happy in the car, this may not present any problems but often as a dog ages, circumstances change and you should think about whether or not a journey or change of environment will be as well tolerated as it once was. Unless you know that he will be happy in the car, take him on one or two short journeys beforehand to familiarise him with the experience and for you to judge his reaction. See appendix 3 for travelling and holiday destination checklist.

If you decide that the journey or the destination are not suitable for your dog, or if he is very old, you may decide to leave him behind. Ideally someone would be staying in your house and able to look after him there in familiar surroundings. It is not acceptable to have a neighbour popping in 2 or 3 times a day to feed him and let him out. Professional house sitters are available to provide this service but if this is not possible, a friend or relative may be able to have him to stay. Failing this he may have to go to kennels.

## Kennels
Although this can be stressful for an elderly dog, if you have a kennel with which he is familiar he may not be too disturbed. If you are using a kennel for the first time, be sure to look at their facilities.

Check that they will provide his normal food or continue any special dietary requirements, give him any medication, regular exercise and that comfortable kennels with heating are available. Check whether he is covered by insurance when in the kennels, and what the arrangements are for veterinary care in your absence. If you prefer your own vet to see him if required, be sure to make this clear. You will need to ensure that his vaccinations are up to date since being old is not an excuse for letting vaccinations lapse. Although kennel cough is not usually dangerous, elderly dogs with already weakened respiratory systems may be at risk from developing pneumonia. It may be worth requesting additional kennel cough protection from your vet before going to kennels, especially in the summer months.

Remember that looking after an elderly dog, especially a very old or ill one, is a great responsibility. Be sure that whoever gets the job is happy with that responsibility, and up to it. Also, try not to be annoyed with them if anything does go wrong. They will already be upset and feeling guilty, even though whatever has happened may just as likely have occurred had you been at home. Leave specific instructions, and the telephone number of your veterinary surgeon. Discuss whether you want to be told if your dog becomes ill, or even dies, whilst you are away, or would you rather not be told until you return. Contact your vet to ask if you may pay any bills when you return, and to give your consent for any operations, or euthanasia if necessary.

You need not feel obliged to do without holidays because you own an elderly, ailing dog, but if you take all precautions to ensure that he will be comfortable and happy whether travelling with you or staying behind, you can travel and holiday with a clear conscience and a relaxed mind.

# Vaccinations

Boosters are still necessary every year, and your dog shouldn't be allowed to go longer than a year between them. Elderly dogs have failing immune systems, and if anything need more frequent vaccination. A great bonus is that the visit to your vet for a booster is used by him or her as an opportunity to give your dog a thorough examination, and it is a chance for you to voice any worries you have, and ask for any advice that you may need.

# Parasite control

## Internal parasites

Dogs may be infested internally with roundworms and tapeworms.

### Roundworms

Whilst roundworms are mainly a problem in young puppies and pregnant or nursing bitches, adult dogs will pick up the eggs of these worms and a few may develop into adult worms in the bowel. If this happens, even the aged dog may pass eggs from its digestive tract and these can infect humans, particularly children. So regardless of age, it is important to maintain a strict worming programme. Elderly dogs should be wormed every 3 months for roundworm. This can be done with a roundworming preparation, which is usually quite cheap, or a combined wormer, which is more expensive.

### Tapeworms

Tapeworms need to pass through an intermediate host during their life-cycle and with the most common type, this intermediate is the flea. When the tapeworm loses segments, these look like grains of rice and may be seen in a dog's stools or in the fur around his bottom. They are unlikely to be a health risk to an elderly dog, but should be treated nevertheless. Flea control should, of course, also be carried out (see below). One other group of tapeworms which affect dogs have rabbits and other small rodents as their intermediate host whilst another type has sheep. In the latter case, dogs become infected by eating sheep carcasses. Tapewormers or, more usually, combined wormers can be used to treat dogs infested with tapeworms. As a routine, treatment every 6 months should be adequate. If fleas are a problem, or your dog eats any raw meat (including carrion), then more frequent dosing may be required.

## External parasites

Dogs may be infested externally with fleas, ticks, lice and mites. These are all parasites which live in or on the skin and usually, except in the case of ticks, cause a degree of irritation and, occasionally, hair loss or more severe skin disease. They are as commonly found on old dogs as they are on youngsters and may even be more of a problem because of the older dog's often poor personal hygiene.

## Fleas

Fleas may be present in large numbers without causing any symptoms, or they may cause scratching, or more severe skin disease. Allergies to the saliva of fleas are common in dogs, and a major cause of skin disorders. Look for them especially just above the base of the tail. If adult fleas are not seen, flea dirt, comma shaped brown droppings, may be seen. Adult fleas seen on the dog will only represent a small proportion of the flea population in the house. 90 per cent or more are in the form of flea eggs and larvae, present in the dog's bed, and anywhere around the house where the dog may go. An important part of flea treatment, then, is to treat the carpets, furniture and bedding.

Baths and sprays and powders are effective treatments for fleas. Although flea collars can be a useful aid to treatment, they will usually not kill 100 per cent of fleas. A recent development in the battle against fleas is the appearance of 'spot-on' preparations which are dropped onto the necks of dogs once a month. One type is a systemic insecticide which is absorbed into the dog's body and the other spreads over the surface of the dog's skin. A new approach is to feed to the dog monthly a drug which sterilises the fleas and interrupts their life-cycle.

## Ticks

Ticks are commonly found on dogs, especially from spring to autumn and are spread by sheep, deer and small mammals such as hedgehogs. As ticks will drop off when they have finished feeding on the dog (after a week to 10 days) and are unlikely to attach themselves to you or any other pets once full, they may safely be left if not irritating the dog. If one is annoying your dog, or is in a sensitive place, or if many are present, you may wish to remove them. It is probably better to ask your veterinary surgeon for the best advice as to how to do this.

## Lice

Lice are most common in puppies and kennelled dogs and are visible to the naked eye as are their eggs (nits), stuck to hairs. As they live and breed on dogs, and can only live for a few days off dogs, which limits their ability to spread, they will not be a problem in many elderly dogs. The best treatment is to give your dog 2 or 3 insecticidal baths and to comb out the nits after treatment. It is not so important to treat the bedding and house as it is when treating fleas, but it would be sensible to wash any bedding at the same time as the dog is bathed.

## Mange mites

Four species of mange mites affect dogs in this country, some living on the surface of the skin and some burrowing through the surface layer. These are not a particular problem of older dogs but veterinary advice should be sought if your suspicions are aroused.

**When treating elderly dogs for ectoparasites, remember that many of the most effective preparations contain organo-phosphorus compounds. These can cause constriction of involuntary muscle, such as is found in lung tissue and the bowel, and they might aggravate respiratory, heart or even bowel conditions. If in doubt, consult your veterinary surgeon for advice.**

# Neutering

You may feel that once your dog has reached old age, the time for considering neutering is long past. If your dog is still entire, however, and just entering old age there may still be benefits to be gained by neutering.

With bitches, disorders of the reproductive system are common in old age (see Chapter 2) and this would seem to be a strong argument for neutering.

The disadvantages of doing this at this stage are often considered to be as follows:

- **Anaesthetic and surgical risk, especially in an elderly bitch**. This should not be taken lightly, but
    a) modern anaesthetic techniques and drugs reduce this risk to a very low level, and
    b) should your bitch need to be neutered at a later date, for instance because she develops a uterine disorder, she will be both older and ill so increasing the risks.
- **Neutering will cause weight gain which is a particular problem for the older dog**. Your bitch will only put on weight if given an energy supply excess to her requirements, and you are in control of that energy supply, her food (see Chapter 4).
- **The possibility of incontinence developing**. Whilst not rare, the condition can usually be successfully treated without ill effects to the bitch.

With dogs, owners are often reluctant to have their male dogs castrated, even if they are perfectly happy to have their bitches spayed (a much more major operation). Cancer of the prostate and testicles and perianal adenomas and hernias are common problems of elderly dogs and are far more likely to occur in entire dogs. The disadvantages versus advantages of undertaking the procedure at this time, as far as anaesthetic risk and weight gain are concerned, are similar to those described for the bitch.

The decision on whether neutering is best for your dog or not should be taken after consultation with your veterinary surgeon, and will involve an assessment of both risks and benefits. The fact is, however, that neutered dogs and bitches live longer on average than entire ones.

For a summary of general care for some common geriatric conditions, see Appendix 4.

# Summary

- Good observation of the aged dog is essential – be aware of changes in appetite, thirst, weight, faeces and urine quantity and quality, skin and coat condition.

- Daily grooming provides valuable contact between you and your dog, and a good opportunity for monitoring health as well as keeping him looking his best.

- Dental care is both practical and rewarding. Keeping your dog's mouth healthy makes a major contribution to good health and makes him more pleasant to know.

- Stress is a serious problem in the aged dog – learn what is likely to stress your dog and how to avoid it.

- Travel and holidays (with or without your dog) need consideration and planning to avoid stressing the older dog.

- Vaccinations and worming are just as important for elderly dogs as for younger ones.

- If your dog is just entering old age it may be worth considering neutering to prevent a range of common disorders.

- Care of elderly dogs involves understanding and adaptation by owners, but can be highly rewarding and should improve quality of life.

# CHAPTER 8
# Nutrition

The many changes in body function which arise in the older dog necessitate a very different approach to feeding compared with his earlier years. This new regime must take into consideration physiological changes such as reduced metabolic rate, reduced digestive capability, sometimes a reduced appetite, the presence of disease in various organs and inefficient use by the body of some nutrients. Unlike younger dogs, a standard diet is unlikely to suit all older dogs and different individuals will have different requirements.

Following are some general considerations which will help us to choose the most suitable diet and feeding regime for the elderly dog. To ease understanding, it may be helpful to briefly describe the basic constituents of food and explain how they are utilised.

## Nutrients

Proteins are made up of long chains of amino acids, the actual components of which account for the different types of protein found. When digested in the body, it is broken down in to individual amino acids which are then used to build new body proteins or provide energy.

When examining the suitability of the protein sources available for the older dog, protein quality is a major consideration. This takes into account:

a) **digestibility** – the ease with which the protein is digested. This is the proportion of protein in the food which can be absorbed by the stomach and intestines, the remainder being lost in the faeces. It varies from as low as 50 per cent for some types of vegetable protein, to about 95 per cent for milk and egg proteins.

b) **amino acid profile** – the amino acids it contains. This is important as there are some which cannot be made in the body (essential amino acids). These must be provided by the protein sources in the dog's diet. Milk and eggs contain the greatest proportion of essential amino acids and cereals the least. Generally, foods which provide protein of high quality are milk and milk products, eggs and white meats. Red meats, offal and cereal have protein of lower quality.

The proportion of protein in a dog's diet is also important and should be about 20 per cent of the dry weight. However, if the protein is of high quality, most adult dogs can manage very well on about half of this and this quantity is usually ideal for elderly dogs. An excess of protein in the diet is likely to result in weight gain, with unhealthy fat being laid down. Deficiency of available protein in the diet may arise as a result of feeding inadequate protein, or, alternatively, protein of poor quality and may cause weight loss, loss of appetite, poor coat quality, increased susceptibility to disease and general poor health. An elderly dog suffering with kidney failure, or some types of liver failure, will, in circumstances of reduced protein intake, have these symptoms aggravated.

# Carbohydrate

Carbohydrates, the main source of energy for the body, are present in foods in three major forms – easily digestible sugars, starches which are easily digested after cooking, and celluloses which are indigestible. Cellulose and other indigestible polysaccharides form dietary fibre and so provide the vitally important roughage content of the food.

Strictly speaking, carbohydrate is not essential to a dog's diet, since it is merely a source of energy which dogs could obtain from protein or fat. In the wild, some dogs eat only meat and fat obtained from the prey they hunt. Our pet dogs are usually fed a high proportion of carbohydrate in the diet as it is a much cheaper source of food. This is usually supplied in the form of biscuit and meal or are added in the processing to dry complete diets. Cooked rice and pasta are other sources of carbohydrate which are more easily digested than cereals.

There is no set recommendation for the percentage of carbohydrate that should be fed in a dog's diet, as a minimum quantity is not required. Dogs are often fed 60-70 per cent of the dry weight of their diet as carbohydrate although a deficiency should not harm a healthy adult dog as long as it receives enough protein and fat to supplement its energy needs. A diet consisting entirely of protein and fat however, is likely to cause digestive disturbances and excess carbohydrate will cause the accumulation of fat. Excess sugar will also contribute to dental disease (see Chapter 2).

# Fat

Fats are the most concentrated source of energy in the diet. They also contain fat-soluble vitamins (A, D and E) and essential fatty acids (EFAs), important for healthy skin and good kidney function (particularly in the elderly dog). Fat is very palatable, and a diet containing large quantities will be attractive to a dog, important in some geriatrics with poor appetite.

Fat is not generally added to the diet as it is usually present in the meat portion of the food in sufficient quantities to provide the nutrients required. Dogs are also able to synthesise some EFAs from the constituents of vegetable oils hence many owners add a teaspoon of cooking oil to a dog's meal once or twice a week. Elderly dogs may have a reduced capacity for synthesising EFAs, and it may prove more helpful to use a EFA containing dietary supplement.

The recommended allowance of fat in the diet is 5 per cent of the dry weight, but less would suffice as long as the sufficient EFAs can be synthesised from oil supplements. If an elderly dog has a poor appetite, a fat rich diet provides a more readily available source of energy.

# Energy

As has been described, energy in itself is not a specific nutrient, being supplied as an essential product of the protein, fat and carbohydrate in the diet. Too little energy in the diet will cause weight loss and poor function of the body's organs, and eventually an inability to maintain body temperature, while excess will be stored as fat, leading to obesity with all its attendant problems. Energy is obtained from the various dietary sources by oxidising ('burning') the food, the amount of energy available being a function of the digestibility of the food and the efficiency of the body at oxidising it. The energy produced by a food is its calorie content which we see noted on the packets of foodstuffs, and is measured in kilo calories (kcal).

As a rule the dietary sources of energy produce the following energy (weights are all dry weight):

| | |
|---|---|
| 1g of *carbohydrate* provides | 3.75 kcal |
| 1g of *protein* provides | 4 kcal |
| 1g of *fat* provides | 9 kcal |

As a rough guide, canned dog food provides about 100 kcal per 100g (wet weight), and mixer biscuit about 350 kcal per 100g.

Table 8.1 gives the basic daily energy requirements for adult dogs (this does not take account of requirements for working or breeding). Neutering and increasing old age will reduce these requirements by up to 20 per cent for each factor. Bitches also tend to have a lower energy requirement than dogs.

| Body weight (kg) | Daily energy requirement (kcal) |
|---|---|
| 5 | 436 |
| 10 | 739 |
| 15 | 1003 |
| 20 | 1254 |
| 25 | 1478 |
| 30 | 1690 |
| 35 | 1901 |
| 40 | 2099 |

**Table 8.1** Daily energy requirement guide for adult dog maintenance

## Minerals

Dogs require about 20 different minerals in their diet with young growing dogs requiring most and elderly dogs considerably less. Some are needed in only tiny quantities and excess intake of some be toxic, disrupting the body's metabolic balance or aggravating existing disease.

Minerals have three main uses:

1) Structural components of bone and teeth (calcium, phosphorus and magnesium)
2) Soluble salts controlling fluid balance (sodium, chloride, potassium, magnesium and phosphorus)
3) In enzymes and other proteins (eg iron in haemoglobin)

Most proprietary diets fed to dogs will contain adequate quantities of minerals although home cooked diets may prove deficient in one or other. Meat, for instance is seriously deficient in calcium, and a dog eating an exclusively meat diet will become deficient.

# Vitamins

Vitamins are essential compounds required in very small quantities for normal body function and health. Most normal diets will provide sufficient of all the vitamins required (note that vitamin C is not required in the dog's diet), but once again a home prepared diet may be deficient in one or more vitamins particularly since overcooking will destroy several vitamins. Home made diets may also contain excessive amounts of certain vitamins which can cause adverse effects such as bone malformation (vitamin A) and calcium deposits in soft tissues (vitamin D) so care should be taken when supplementing the diet with vitamin preparations or foods rich in these vitamins.

# Roughage (fibre)

As described under carbohydrate, roughage is the indigestible portion of carbohydrates in a dog's food which passes through the bowel essentially unchanged. It serves to provide bulk, and acts as a sponge, absorbing fluid and so helping to maintain normal faecal consistency, reducing the tendency to constipation by keeping stools moist and soft, and diarrhoea, by soaking up excess water. Although this is particularly valuable in the older dog, these dogs often suffer with a poor appetite, and a high fibre diet means that fewer useful nutrients can be taken in. Older dogs should therefore eat a diet with less than 4 per cent (dry weight) fibre although those carrying excess weight will benefit from the reduced energy yielding/high fibre food with a higher fibre content of around 10 per cent.

# Water

Water should also be included in the list of nutrients required by the dog since it is the nutrient without which a dog can survive for the least time. It is required in some form for almost all bodily functions, and makes up a large percentage of the body's mass being lost from the dog in urine and faeces, and by evaporation from the respiratory tract particularly when panting. Water is taken into the body in food and as drinking water and normally a dog will drink as much as it requires. Dogs fed on moist food, however, such as proprietary tinned meat, will require less drinking water than those on dry complete foods although the requirements of individual animals may vary greatly. Assuming good health, there is little need to be concerned if a dog seems to drink very little as long as plenty of fresh drinking water is available at all times. An average, healthy adult dog of about 15 kg in weight will require around 1 litre of water per day and if fed on dry food, virtually all of this will need to come from his drinking bowl whereas a dog fed on moist food may only need half of this.

Dogs which are unwell may become dehydrated because they have a greater requirement for water or because they feel too unwell to drink what they need. These dogs need to be encouraged to drink and force fed if necessary. Vomiting and diarrhoea, chronic kidney failure and diabetes mellitus are all conditions which increase the loss of water.

# Feeding elderly dogs

## General considerations

Aged dogs may suffer from a range of conditions which makes it hard to suggest one diet that is suitable for all. In general:

1) Elderly dogs will need less energy in the diet because of a falling metabolic rate, and it is important to avoid obesity.
2) Feeding two or three meals a day will help the aged dog's less efficient digestive system to cope with breaking down the food and absorbing nutrients, and may aid bowel control. It may also encourage eating if appetite is reduced.
3) Restricted amounts of high quality protein will reduce the stress on the kidneys which may have started to fail.
4) The diet should be highly digestible unless the dog is overweight, when extra fibre is advisable.
5) Reduced salt in the diet will lower the incidence of high blood pressure and reduce the strain on the heart and circulatory system.
6) Dogs which have a poor appetite may either eat insufficient to provide their daily vitamin requirement, or prefer to eat specific foods which fail to provide a balance of vitamins; these dogs, and those having their diets controlled by their owners may need vitamin supplements. Supplementing the diet with B vitamins helps stimulate appetite, aids energy metabolism and reduces the incidence of anaemia; extra vitamin A and E may be helpful for skin, muscle and eyes, but care should be taken when supplementing fat soluble vitamins (A, D, E and K) as overdose may have toxic effects – a proprietary vitamin tablet or powder may be used at the dose recommended but no more.

7) The addition of essential fatty acids is very useful to keep skin and coat in good condition – your veterinary surgeon will be able to provide a balanced supplement.

8) As many elderly dogs suffer from conditions which increase their water loss, it is especially important to ensure that fresh drinking water is available at all times.

## Practical feeding

As the owner of an ageing dog, you have the option of feeding commercial dog foods, home prepared foods, prescription diets or a mixture of these. Table 8.2 shows the recommended levels of the main nutrients for elderly dogs, and the nutrient content of some foods. It can be seen that the prescription diet for geriatric dogs closely matches the recommended levels.

| Nutrients | | Recommended allowance per 100g dry food intake | Content per 100g dry matter | | |
| --- | --- | --- | --- | --- | --- |
| | | | Meaty canned food | Meaty canned food/biscuit 3:1 | Prescription geriatric diet[1] |
| Energy | kcals | ≥ 374 | 444 | 432 | 378 |
| Protein | g | 14 – 21 | 44.4 | 24.3 | 14 |
| Fat | g | > 10 | 22.2 | 16.2 | 9.5 |
| Fibre | g | < 10 | | | 1.2 |
| Calcium | g | 0.5 – 0.8 | 1.94 | 1.62 | 0.54 |
| Phosphorus | g | 0.4 – 0.7 | 1.39 | 1.08 | 0.33 |
| Sodium chloride | g | 0.2 – 0.4 | | | 0.25 |

1. Canine Low Protein Diet (Pedigree Petfoods)

**Table 8.2** Recommended nutrient allowances for aged dogs, and nutrients provided by some foods

Commercial diets have the advantages of ease and convenience, long storage times and a good balance of nutrients and vitamins. Although a specific prescription diet may not be suitable for every older dogs, alternative prescription diets are available to take note of any specific medical requirements. Home prepared diets have the advantage that you can tailor them to the individual dog's needs, but they are time-consuming, can't be stored easily and may be deficient in vitamins and minerals.

Further considerations are listed in Table 8.3.

| Food | Advantages | Disadvantages |
|---|---|---|
| **Commercial foods** | Convenient<br>Long storage times<br>Contain range of nutrients<br>Consistent composition | Nutrient profile may not match that recommended for every geriatric |
| Canned food | Good palatability<br>Highly digestible | Some dogs are prone to diarrhoea on canned diets |
| Semi-moist food | Convenient – can be fed alone<br>Low odour, no mess<br>Good digestibility | Less palatable than canned food |
| Dry complete diets – cereal based | Ease of use<br>Can be fed alone<br>Low cost<br>Energy rich – good for dogs with reduced appetite | Relatively low palatability<br>Relatively low digestibility<br>Energy rich – bad for inactive or obese dogs |
| Dry complete diets – extruded pellets | Ease of use<br>Can be fed alone<br>Usually better quality protein than cereal based foods<br>Usually better palatability and digestibility than cereal based foods<br>Low faecal bulk<br>Energy rich – good for dogs with reduced appetite | May not be palatable to some dogs<br>Tend to be a little more expensive<br>Energy rich – bad for inactive or obese dogs |
| Mixer biscuits | Cheap source of energy and bulk | Must be fed with meat or canned food<br>Low palatability |
| **Home prepared diets** | Highly palatable<br>Can be tailored to individual dogs' requirements<br>Usually low salt | Inconvenient to prepare<br>May be deficient in certain nutrients<br>Poor storage times |

**Table 8.3** Features of some foods

If you are using home-prepared diets for your dog, the food should be cooked so to reduce the chance of bacterial infection, worm and other parasite infestation, and to increase digestibility although overcooking may reduce the vitamin content. A mixture of different foods will be necessary to provide a balance of nutrients and you

| Food item | Source of | Deficient in | Comment |
|---|---|---|---|
| Meat | Good quality protein, fat, iron, some B vitamins | Calcium, iodine, vitamins A and D, biotin | Good palatability and digestibility |
| Tripe | Protein, fat | Calcium, other minerals, vitamins | |
| Liver | Protein, fat, fat soluble vitamins, B vitamins | Calcium, other minerals | Excess liver can cause disease related to vitamin overdose, especially vitamin A |
| Fish (white) | Good quality protein, iodine, calcium (in bones) | Fat soluble vitamins, fat | May be less palatable than meats |
| Fish (oily) | Protein, fat, fat soluble vitamins | | |
| Milk and dairy products | Most nutrients | Iron, vitamin D | Some dogs cannot digest milk sugar and may develop diarrhoea if given milk<br>Good digestibility |
| Eggs | Most nutrients | Niacin | Good digestibility<br>Raw egg white contains a substance which makes biotin unavailable to dogs<br>Raw eggs may cause diarrhoea |
| Cereals | Energy, some minerals, some poor quality protein, some B vitamins, roughage | Fat, fat soluble vitamins, essential fatty acids | Mainly suitable as cheap source of energy, and bulk |
| Fats and oils | Energy, fat soluble vitamins, essential fatty acids | All other nutrients | Highly palatable and digestible<br>Used cooking fat should not be given to dogs as it contains harmful peroxides and other toxic materials |
| Vegetables | Roughage, B vitamins | Protein, fat | Of limited value to dogs<br>Useful as bulking agents for obese dogs |

**Table 8.4** Characteristics of various food types

may need to provide a vitamin and mineral supplement to ensure a satisfactory supply of these essentials. Table 8.4 describes the items which may be used in a home-prepared diet.

A good basic home-prepared diet for elderly dogs consists of a high quality (white meat) source of protein, easily digestible carbohydrate such as rice or pasta, some green vegetables, corn oil and a vitamin/mineral supplement. The actual constituents can be altered depending on whether the dog is losing weight or, indeed, overweight, and whether it is suffering from a specific disease or condition requiring special needs.

## Other considerations when feeding

Warming the food to room temperature or slightly above may increase the palatability of the food and improves the odour. Smell is important in stimulating a dog's appetite and the aged dog's sense of smell may be impaired.

If you have more than one dog, it may be better to feed the old one on her own, so that she doesn't feel threatened, can relax and doesn't bolt her food. Younger dogs will eat more rapidly, and may steal some of the old dog's food once they have eaten their own. In some cases, however, the competition of having other dogs eating nearby will stimulate an old dog to eat.

If an elderly dog is suffering from arthritis and other aches and pains, lowering her neck to a food bowl may be uncomfortable. Placing the bowl on a low stool or similar object will make feeding easier.

Elderly dogs often have reduced control of their bowel, and may have accidents in the house. If this is the case, it may be useful to feed the greater part of her food earlier in the day, and only to give a snack at night, so as to lessen the pressure on the bowels.

# Special diets

Several of the conditions of old age can be treated or controlled by diet. Normal tinned and dry proprietary foods are unlikely to match the nutritional requirements of these medical conditions but in addition to simple geriatric diets discussed earlier, your veterinary surgery will be able to supply canned and dry prescription diets to treat a variety of conditions. The following are some of the conditions that can be helped by diet, and the aims of feeding. Basic recipes for home-produced diets are also given. Vitamins and minerals will usually need to be added to these.

## Obesity (see also Chapter 4)

As we have mentioned, obesity is a serious and common problem in elderly dogs. We have described the method of dieting an obese dog. It is worth remembering that a slow, steady loss of weight is healthier for the old dog. It is also important not to restrict nutrients too greatly as the dog may become deficient in protein and vitamins. Major reduction in the carbohydrate part of the diet is the best method of weight control.

It is also important when feeding the elderly dog to remember that it is likely to have an energy surplus in its diet because of its lower metabolic rate and decreasing activity levels. This should be taken into consideration, and the intake of calories strictly monitored.

| Aims | Reasons | Achieved by |
|---|---|---|
| Restrict protein intake | Reduce toxic by-products of protein break-down (urea) | Feed small quantities of good quality protein (eggs, white meat/fish, lean mince) Chronic renal failure – feed 2.2 g/kg body weight protein/day Severe renal failure – feed 1.3 g/kg body weight protein/day |
| Supply energy rich diet | Prevents the dog breaking down its own muscle mass to provide energy Reduce use of dietary protein for energy | Feed highly digestible carbohydrate (cooked rice, potato, cereal) Add fat/oil to the diet |
| Adequate sodium supply | Compensate for sodium loss via kidneys Encourage water intake | Add salt to diet – preferably half sodium chloride (0.1mg/kg body weight) and half sodium bicarbonate (0.2mg/kg)/day to avoid acidosis |
| Control potassium intake | Diseased kidneys unable to excrete potassium | Restrict protein (high protein foods usually potassium rich) |
| Adequate water intake | Compensate for increased loss via kidneys | Plenty of fresh drinking water |
| Supplement B vitamins | Compensate for loss via kidneys Help energy metabolism Stimulate appetite Help counteract anaemia | Give vitamin B complex supplement (tablets, yeast, Marmite) |

# Chronic kidney failure

If weight loss occurs, the low protein diet may need to be supplemented. The best method of doing this is to supply egg protein (scrambled eggs are useful). Because egg protein is of the highest biological quality, less will need to be added to the diet than if another source of protein were used.

Because patients suffering from kidney failure often have a poor appetite and suffer from vomiting, the diet should be palatable, and be split into two or three meals a day. White meats are palatable, easy on the stomach and supply good quality protein.

## Sample recipe:
115g chicken
1 large egg (hard boiled)
2 cups cooked rice (salted)
3 slices white bread
1 teaspoon calcium carbonate
1-2 teaspoons corn oil
*Produces about 600g (1$\frac{1}{4}$ lb)*

# Heart disease

| Aims | Reasons | Achieved by |
| --- | --- | --- |
| Restrict sodium intake | Reduce hypertension – aggravates congestive heart failure | Feed fresh meats, fish, egg yolk, potato, pasta, rice, vegetables<br>Avoid offal, cereals, bread, butter, whole egg, treats, proprietary foods |
| Keep stomach size small | A large stomach presses on the diaphragm, forcing it forwards. This further impairs cardiac function | Feed several small meals daily |
| Avoid obesity | Aggravates all aspects of heart failure<br>Dogs will be less active, so more prone to obesity | Restrict energy intake |

Low salt diets are not usually very palatable to dogs. Palatability can be improved by roasting or even frying.

## Example recipe:
115g lean meat
2 cups cooked rice without salt
1 tablespoon vegetable oil
2 teaspoons dicalcium phosphate
Salt free vitamin and mineral supplement
*Produces about 450g (1 lb)*

## Liver disease

| Aims | Reasons | Achieved by |
|---|---|---|
| Restrict protein intake | Reduce need for detoxification of protein break-down products Prevent ammonia toxicity | Feed small amounts of high quality protein (as for kidney failure). Avoid offal, meat by-products and other poor quality protein. Feed 2–3 g/kg body weight protein |
| Provide easily digested energy sources | Reduce workload for liver – normally produces and stores glucose/glycogen Reduce need for protein as energy source | Feed starch – rice, potato, pasta Avoid coarse grain cereals (present in many dog foods) |
| Restrict fat | Fat digestion and metabolism are impaired | Feed low fat foods, and avoid fatty supplements About 6 per cent of calorie intake should be in the form of fat |
| Control sodium intake | Reduce water retention – dogs with liver failure may develop ascites (fluid in the abdomen) | Avoid proprietary foods and high salt foods/treats Aim for less than 100mg/100g of diet (dry matter) |
| Reduce stress on liver | The liver is necessary for digestion and metabolism of most nutrients – after a large meal it will be working very hard | Split ration into several small meals (4–6 daily) |
| Supplement vitamins | Low vitamin levels are common in liver disease | Especially supplement vitamin B complex. Also vitamins C, D and K |

# Summary

- A standard diet is unlikely to suit all older dogs and it is important to consider changes in diet which may prolong and improve the quality of your dog's life.

- Many of the conditions of old age can be treated or at least controlled by diet.

# CHAPTER 9
# Veterinary care

With luck, your ageing dog will enjoy the best of health but the likelihood is that she will need a certain amount of veterinary attention during her latter years. Even healthy dogs should be checked every now and then. Your veterinary surgeon is the person best qualified to advise you on the care and health of your dog, and he or she will always be happy to give you that advice if asked. Always seek the earliest treatment if you notice any signs of disorder (see Chapter 2), as this will give the best chance to cure or control a disease. Don't sit on a problem hoping that it will go away – they seldom do. It may be that you will be told that there is nothing to worry about, and you will be able to relax. It might be that the news is not so good, but remember, early diagnosis doesn't shorten a dog's life or increase its suffering.

# The importance of regular check-ups

Most well cared for dogs of all ages will receive at least one veterinary check each year, when they have their annual booster vaccinations. This is an important visit, not just for the protection which vaccination affords, but also because it is a valuable point of contact between you and your vet. Veterinary science changes and advances at a rapid pace. In your dog's lifetime many important discoveries and new ideas will be put forward. A vet is able to pass on relevant information when he sees his clients, but if they are not seen regularly, the opportunity for giving much valuable advice will be missed. New drugs and diets appear each year, and these are most likely to be of use to your geriatric dog, with the possible disorders he may suffer from.

Elderly dogs would benefit from more frequent health checks. The interval varies from dog to dog, but may range from six monthly for a healthy dog, to monthly for a dog with advanced heart disease. Frequent checks give the best opportunity to pick up fresh disorders and monitor the progress of established disease. The response to medication also needs to be checked, as well as the presence of any side effects.

Check-ups also allow you the chance to ask any questions you wish about your dog's health and care. Be sure to bring to the vet's attention any changes you have noticed, especially in thirst, appetite, weight and exercise tolerance. All lumps and bumps that you have found should be examined. In between checks, keep notes on your dog's health, response to medication and any changes in behaviour. Make a note of lumps in the skin when you first notice them, together with an estimate of their size. This is useful to you as it is often hard to be precise about when something was first noticed, and whether it has actually changed or not with time.

## What does a health check involve?

To begin with your dog should be given a thorough physical examination. She will be examined externally, checking all the points that you will hopefully be monitoring at home, such as dental disease, coat and skin condition, eyes and ears, any skin growths and mobility. More detailed examination of eyes and ears may be given, checking of heart and lungs with a stethoscope, palpation of the abdomen to detect internal tumours and changes in size or shape of internal organs. Limbs may be manipulated to find signs of arthritis.

Following the physical examination and discussion with you, further tests or procedures may be recommended. They may also be advised routinely, perhaps yearly, to help with detection of disease before any symptoms or physical changes occur. Some of these further investigations are described below.

## Urine analysis

This is quick, easily performed, cheap and can be very informative. It would be sensible to always take a urine sample with you if you are consulting a veterinary surgeon, whether for a routine check-up or because your dog is ill. Diabetes mellitus or insipidus, cystitis, prostate disorders, liver and kidney disease are examples of disorders which may be picked up by urine examination.

A sample collected from your dog when she first urinates in the morning is most useful, assuming that she hasn't eaten overnight. If she has developed an increased thirst, it may be useful to deprive her of water overnight before collecting the sample, but you should consult your vet first in case this isn't safe. Prepare a container to contain the sample. Waterproof glass and plastic jars (eg tablet bottles) are suitable. They should be cleaned thoroughly and allowed to dry. The sample should be obtained directly from your dog, to avoid the possibility of contamination. Only a small amount is needed. Dogs usually present no problem, but collecting from bitches can be more difficult. Try using a clean, shallow tray, a foil pie dish for instance, and slip this under her once she has started. The sample should be collected mid-stream to give a true representation of the urine.

## Faeces analysis

Your vet may want to examine your dog's faeces for consistency, colour, and the presence of mucus or blood. Faeces can also be checked for the presence of worm eggs, though this is unlikely to be necessary with aged dogs.

## Blood tests

A blood count can help detect anaemia, bacterial and viral infections, immune disorders and some types of cancer.

A blood chemistry profile assesses the function of internal organs, and can help to diagnose certain disorders such as diabetes mellitus. If you dog suffers from heart, liver or kidney failure, regular blood tests will help monitor the progress of these diseases, together with the response to any treatment. Blood tests will also help to check whether any medication that your dog is taking is affecting internal organ function.

## X-rays

X-rays can provide a great deal of information useful in assessing the health of the elderly dog. Heart size, lung diseases (including tumours), changes in size of abdominal organs, skeletal disorders (eg arthritis, slipped discs) and cancers may all be detected with x-ray examination. It is usually necessary to use a general anaesthetic or deep sedation for this procedure, both for the safety of veterinary staff (patients should only be held for x-rays in exceptional circumstances) and to keep the dog still so that the best quality picture can be obtained.

## Ultrasound examination

Some veterinary practices now own or have access to ultrasound machines. These enable assessments of internal organ size, detection of some internal masses, and a dynamic picture of heart function.

## Electrocardiogram (ECG)

An ECG may be taken to help assess heart function. Enlargement of heart chambers, disorders of heart rhythm, and some systemic diseases can all be detected. This is a relatively quick procedure, usually performed without the need for sedation, and done while you wait.

# What conditions can be treated?

Disease cures are usually limited to those conditions caused by bacterial or viral infection, or nutritional imbalances, or conditions which can be corrected by surgery, including tumours, bowel obstructions and foreign bodies.

Most of the diseases of old age are consequences of the loss of tissue, reduced efficiency or altered function of various organs. Cure of these conditions is not usually a possibility, but alleviation of the symptoms and slowing or arresting the progress of the disease is. Many disorders can be managed well enough to totally abolish the symptoms, which is the next best thing to a cure. Most important is to reduce discomfort and suffering to the minimum, and prolong life if possible.

Arthritis, heart disease, respiratory disease, kidney failure, liver failure, diabetes mellitus, hormonal incontinence and dental disease are amongst the diseases of old age that can be very successfully controlled.

The treatment of cancer, if possible, will usually involve surgery to remove tumours. The earlier that cancer is detected and operated upon, the better the chance of success. If treatment is delayed, then the tumour will have more chance of spreading to other organs, and even if the original mass is completely removed, secondaries will appear. It is important to check for regrowth of tumours once they have been removed, and to look out for the symptoms of secondary tumours. Your vet will advise you on this. If surgical elimination of the tumour is not possible, then some other form of therapy may be advised. This is unlikely to produce a cure, but may bring about remission and an increased life expectancy. Chemotherapy is relatively commonly used. It is possible to attempt aggressive cancer therapy with chemotherapeutic agents, but we must consider whether it is fair on the dog. Unlike us, dogs cannot understand that the ill effects of treatment that they suffer may be worthwhile in the long run. Before embarking on aggressive therapy we should consider the side effects, the dog's life expectancy (disregarding the tumour) and the chance of success. It is often possible to use drugs which are well tolerated by dogs, and will not cause distress.

# Safety of treatment

## Is treatment necessary?

Owners sometimes seem reluctant to start a dog on treatment for the diseases of old age, especially if the symptoms don't appear to be serious. There may be several reasons for this.

### 1) The disease doesn't seem to worry the dog.
Dogs have no concept about the possibility of their disorder being improved by treatment. They accept their condition and degree of comfort as it is each day, and try to get on with life as normal. This doesn't mean that they are not suffering, nor that they wouldn't appreciate treatment. Two examples of commonly neglected disorders are arthritis and dental disease. If a dog is showing symptoms of arthritis, such as stiffness when rising, a limp or reduced exercise tolerance, then it is in some degree of discomfort. If treatment banishes

or improves the symptoms, then it is also improving the dog's level of comfort. Similarly with dental disease, just because a dog continues to eat and doesn't complain about its sore teeth or gums, this doesn't mean that he isn't suffering pain. Any of us who have experienced a tooth abscess can testify to the discomfort, but a dog isn't able to tell us about it.

## 2) The side effects of drugs

It is undeniable that certain drugs will cause side effects in dogs, although these are probably less common and fewer in number than people think. Typically, the drugs used to treat old dogs may cause gastro-intestinal upsets, or aggravate liver or kidney disease. Your vet will be perfectly happy to discuss any possible side effects and how to minimise them, but if a disease needs treatment, then that treatment should be used. Veterinary surgeons are used to balancing the benefits and drawbacks of treatment and won't knowingly cause your dog more problems than they sort out.

Remember:

i) Earlier treatment usually enables lower doses of drugs to be used. By waiting until symptoms are severe, higher doses, more likely to cause problems, will be necessary.

ii) Modern drugs and dosage regimes are intended to reduce the possibility of side effects. Often it is possible to use no risk, or extremely low risk medications to treat conditions.

ii) Even if side effects are a serious risk, with the possibility of shortening your dog's life span, from the dog's point of view it may be better to enjoy a short, comfortable and mobile life than to endure a longer painful and sedentary one.

## 3) Cost of drugs and special diets

A few drugs will work out expensive, more so if several drugs are needed to treat the same or separate conditions. The majority are cheap to use in the long term. If cost is a major stumbling block, then explain this to your vet, who may be able to suggest an acceptable cheaper alternative.

Special diets, whether bought complete or home prepared, are going to be more expensive than standard proprietary food. When considering the cost of a prescription diet, for instance, remember to deduct the cost of the food you would feed in any case, the drugs you might not need to administer, and the titbits you won't be allowed to feed!

If you have had the foresight to insure your dog when it was younger, you will find that much of the cost of drugs is covered, and usually the difference in price between prescription food and normal dog food.

### 4) The nuisance of administering drugs or altering diet

In taking on a dog as a pet and companion we make a commitment. It is our responsibility to make sure that we do all we can to maintain our dog's health and comfort. When we first take home our little bundle of fun, it is hard to appreciate that in 9 or 10 years it will be an old dog, but we must think about this and be prepared to fulfil our obligations later in life. Dogs are faithful, rewarding and uncomplaining companions who deserve a little effort on our part when they require it. Once a routine of tablet administration is established, it becomes almost effortless. If preparing special diets is too time consuming or not practical, commercial prescription diets are available to suit every disorder.

# What if my aged dog needs to have a general anaesthetic or surgery?

We are rightly concerned about the effects on our dogs of anaesthesia. It is sensible to be aware that there is a risk involved whenever a dog is anaesthetised, no matter how minor the operation or how short the anaesthesia. This risk should be put in perspective, however. It is extremely rare for anaesthetic accidents to occur. Discounting routine surgery, such as neutering, a greater proportion of dogs aged 8 and over are going to need surgery compared to dogs under that age. Dental treatment, x-ray investigations, tumour removals, pyometra surgery (requiring ovariohysterectomy) and castration as preventative therapy (eg for prostate disease) are all much more common in the older dog. Nevertheless the incidence of problems and deaths under anaesthesia for these procedures is very small. Your vet will warn you when he or she considers a procedure a particular risk for your dog.

Even if your dog seems very elderly, and if it is known that there is a degree of risk in proceeding with surgery, if your vet has advised the procedure it will be because it is in your dog's best interest, and it is sensible to allow the surgery to be performed. If, for example, you have a 13 year old dog with a small tumour on its leg, your vet may advise you to have it removed. You might be reluctant to take the risk of the general anaesthetic at this time. You decide to wait and see if the lump causes problems. However, it may then become unavoidable to excise the tumour a year later, because it has grown large and is uncomfortable and interfering with the function of the leg. The risks have now soared, not just because the dog is older, but also because the operation will be more complicated and consequently longer, and the tumour may have already spread, meaning that surgery may not be enough to cure the problem. Tackle problems early, because while disorders generally get worse, dogs just get older.

## How can the risks of surgery be minimised?

i) Your veterinary surgeon will take special precautions when performing procedures under general anaesthetic on your elderly dog. New types of anaesthetic are shorter acting and have less adverse effects on the liver and kidneys. These are particularly suited to aged dogs. He may administer an intravenous drip. The depth of anaesthesia and the length of the procedure will be kept to an absolute minimum. The dog will be constantly monitored whilst asleep to pick up any adverse signs. Of course all these precautions are taken with any dog undergoing surgery, but their especial application to elderly dogs may mean that they often recover more quickly from surgery than younger dogs.

Post-operative administration of antibiotics will help to reduce the risk of secondary infections which might become established while your dog's resistance is low.

ii) Your vet may carry out a full pre-operative health check. He may perform a physical examination, but a blood test to check blood chemistry and a blood count may help to pinpoint specific areas of concern, or even show if surgery should be delayed until other problems are resolved or improved. Any infections or organ failure detected can be treated prior to the anaesthetic. An ECG can be performed to help assess the condition and function of the heart, and any disorders treated.

iii) So that operating time can be kept to a minimum, have problems corrected at the earliest opportunity. Check your dog regularly for any abnormalities, such as bad teeth or skin growths, and seek advice on them. If surgery is then advised, don't delay unnecessarily.

iv) Obesity is an important cause of increased anaesthetic risk. Equally, debilitated dogs or those receiving inadequate nutrition are at an increased risk. Ensure that your dog is kept in as healthy a condition as possible, and at its correct weight.

# What if I am unable to get my dog to the surgery?

There will be times when it proves hard to take an elderly dog to the surgery. A large dog suffering badly from arthritis, or in a state of collapse is not easy to manoeuvre into the car and then into the surgery. You may feel that it is less distressing for your dog if it doesn't have to travel to your vet.

Almost all veterinary surgeons are prepared to carry out house visits. Please remember, though that these are not always convenient, and although the vet will try to be with you as soon as possible, he may be dealing with other patients and be unable to get away. If the reason for wanting an examination is not urgent, then give the surgery plenty of notice. Telephone the day before, or as early as possible in the morning, and be prepared to be at home during working hours. If you yourself cannot be at home and you have to ask a friend to meet the vet, please be sure to write down exactly what the problem is, how long it has worried you and any observations about your dog that you have made. For a veterinary surgeon the information gained by talking to you is often as important as the physical examination of the patient.

If you feel that your dog needs urgent attention, it is almost always quicker to take her to the surgery, even if inconvenient. By the time a vet has managed to free himself and then drive to and find your house, much valuable time may have passed. Call the surgery to explain the problem, and ask what they advise.

Although house visits are convenient for you, for any serious problems your dog will be better cared for at the surgery, where the full range of medications, investigative equipment and support is available. The drugs and equipment which can be carried on a visit are extremely limited. If your dog is very ill, the vet is most likely to want to return her to the surgery in any case.

Remember that you must expect to pay a visit fee as well as any consultation and treatment fee.

## Using medication and following veterinary advice

Treatment of many of the diseases of old age will involve the giving of long term medication, usually in the form of oral tablets or liquids. It is important to use this medication exactly as advised by your veterinary surgeon in order to get the best benefit and value from it, and to minimise any side-effects. Aspects of medication particularly important to the older dog include whether or not there may be interaction of one medication with others, whether or not the course is the complete treatment, how important it is if one or two doses are missed and whether it is possible to alter the dose according to the response, or must the stated dose be strictly adhered to?

When your dog is put on a course of treatment, your vet will usually ask you to return for follow up consultations. It is important to return at the time asked, especially if only enough drugs are given to last to the next appointment. A dog will often appear to be back to normal after a short course of drugs, but when the course is finished, the problem may gradually reappear. Apart from being bad for your dog, this can involve you in extra expense, if the vet needs to keep restarting courses of treatment from the beginning. If you know that you are going to be unable to keep your appointment, let the surgery know so that they can supply you with sufficient drugs, if necessary, to last until you are able to return.

Veterinary surgeons are in a privileged position in that they are able not only to prescribe drugs, but also to dispense them. In order to maintain this position, they must adhere strictly to the laws governing the use and supply of drugs. In practice this means that drugs are unlikely to be able to be given out without examining the dog and ensuring that they are required. Owners often find this frustrating but there are good reasons for the drugs having restricted availability and you must respect this.

## Is veterinary treatment affordable?

Medical and surgical treatment for your dog may sometimes appear to be expensive. The problem for the veterinary profession is that our national health service, however much maligned, does a wonderful job in providing 'free' treatment for all. Of course nothing is free, and we all pay for the health service through our taxes. Pet health insurance is an excellent way of ensuring that you will be able to afford whatever treatment you dog needs but you need to think about this before you dog becomes aged, as many insurers won't take on elderly dogs because they need more treatment. Never be afraid or embarrassed to ask your vet how much treatment is likely to cost. Although it is not always possible to be completely accurate in estimating cost, a good idea of what is involved can be gained. If you feel that you are unable to afford the treatment needed, discuss it with your vet. He may be able to suggest an alternative, or suggest ways of spreading the payment. He may be able to suggest charities who could help with the bill, or even refer you to a surgery run by a charity such as the PDSA (People's Dispensary for Sick Animals). The main concern of veterinary surgeons is the welfare of your dog, and although it is necessary to charge for providing treatment, no vet will allow your dog to suffer unnecessarily.

### Keep your costs down by:
1) Seeking the earliest possible treatment for problems – the longer they have to develop, the more protracted and costly the cure
2) Ensure that you do all you can to keep your dog in good health – good nutrition and home health care pay dividends. A good example is the cleaning of teeth, which can help avoid or delay dental surgery.
3) Take your dog to the surgery if possible as home visits may be costly.
4) Avoid unnecessary emergency calls at night or weekends. If your dog appears ill during the day, seek treatment sooner rather than later.

## Your veterinary surgeon is always available

The veterinary profession is rightly proud of its commitment to provide veterinary care 24 hours a day, 365 days a year. The public is not always aware of this fact, but all practices in this country must provide this emergency cover. Although happy to provide this service, calls out of hours are expensive for you and make demands on vets' private lives. Try not to use the service unnecessarily. Remember, however, that you are the person observing your dog, and you are the one who must decide whether he needs attention urgently or not. If you feel that he needs to be seen, rest assured that your vet will attend.

If your dog does require attention out of hours, be prepared to take him to the surgery if at all possible. As well as a condition being best treated at the surgery, it can be difficult for the vet to find his way to your house in the dark.

# Summary

- Your veterinary surgeon has an important role to play in ensuring a happy, healthy old age for your dog.

- Use your vet more for prevention and early treatment of disease than for emergency treatment of established disorders.

- Ensure that your ageing dog receives regular health checks – at least every 6 months.

- Much can be done to alleviate the symptoms of the diseases of old age.

- If your dog is showing symptoms of a disorder, the chances are that it is in discomfort or feeling unwell, and should be treated. Dogs are unable to tell us how they feel, so we have a serious responsibility to spare them any unnecessary suffering.

- If you are worried about the possible side-effects of drugs, discuss this fully with your vet. If the treatment will significantly improve your dog's quality of life, it should probably be used, even at a slight risk to his health in other ways.

- Modern drugs and techniques, health checks and precautions all make general anaesthesia relatively safe for the geriatric. If a condition requires surgery, the risks of leaving it untreated will far outweigh the risks of anaesthesia.

- Veterinary fees represent good value for money, but can still come as an unpleasant shock. Try to minimise costs to yourself by insurance, early treatment of conditions and good health care at home.

- Remember that your vet is always available when you need him.

# CHAPTER 10
# First aid

If your dog is injured, unwell or poisoned, you should always aim to consult a veterinary surgeon, even if only by 'phone in the first instance. It is as well to have some idea about first aid to enable you to treat minor problems before a vet is seen, or out of surgery hours to tide the dog over (although you may contact a vet at any time if you are worried). The advantage you have as the owner of an aged dog is that by and large she will be more sensible and less reckless than a younger dog. Cuts and fractures from charging around in a headlong fashion, swallowing of stones and other interesting but inappropriate objects, stings and bites from close examination of bad tempered insects – you should be spared all these and more to a certain extent. On the other side of the coin, old bones are more fragile, and poor senses and unsteady legs can make accidents more likely.

This chapter deals with some common problems and emergencies. Some general points to remember in case of emergency are:

1) Keep your vet's 'phone number in a prominent place. Ideally you should have a name disc on your dog with the vet's number engraved on it, so that anyone finding your dog can contact the vet as quickly as possible.
2) Always 'phone the vet first even in a dire emergency. This will ensure that
   i) you are taking the dog to the right surgery
   ii) a vet will actually be present or called in,
   iii) the surgery can have the right equipment ready
   iv) the vet has the opportunity to give (possibly life saving) advice.
3) Ensure that you or others helping do not get bitten.
4) Do not offer any food or drink in case your dog requires a general anaesthetic.

## A-Z of emergencies

### Bites
*Dog bites:* Clean up and control any bleeding. Always consult a vet, as dog bites will become infected.
*Snake bites:* Adders may bite inquisitive dogs, especially in spring when they are sluggish. The characteristic pair of puncture wounds

may be seen, but swelling of the nose/leg may be the only sign seen. Can be dangerous for small dogs. Carry the dog back to the car if possible. Do not apply a tourniquet. Keep the dog calm, and take straight to vet, telephoning en route if possible.

## Bleeding
Small to medium amounts of bleeding, caused by trauma, torn claws, cuts when grooming etc, can be controlled with pressure from a lint pad applied for several minutes. If possible, applying a firm dressing will help. A tight dressing should not be left in place for more than 15 minutes. Dark seeping blood comes from a cut vein. A dressing will usually control this, if the blood vessel is not large. A cut artery will spurt bright red blood in pulses. Firm pressure and possibly a tourniquet will be required. A vet will need to examine the source of bleeding.

## Burns
*Heat burns*: Apply very cold running water in copious quantities, seek veterinary treatment. Elderly dogs can be badly burnt by lying too close to fires, when their coats get very hot before the dog itself feels the heat. The coat can also hide the extent of the burn.
*Chemical burns*: Wash off the chemical as quickly as possible. Contact the vet.

## Chemicals
May be accidentally or maliciously sprayed into eyes. Wash with profuse amounts of tepid water. Seek veterinary advice.

## Choking
*Foreign body in the throat*: Commonly a ball that is too small. **Very urgent**. Contact vet and get to surgery as soon as possible. If unable to breathe attempt to remove. Difficult to do without pushing it further in as saliva makes the ball slippery, and it is often well wedged in. Be careful not to get bitten. If you can't hold the ball via the mouth, feel for it from outside the throat, just behind the angle of the jaw. Pressure forwards at this point may dislodge the ball, or move it forwards enough to grasp it from the mouth.
*Across the roof of the mouth*: Usually a bone or stick. If you can grasp it with pliers (without getting bitten) push it gently backwards towards the throat until free, then remove it. If the dog won't allow this, a vet will need to remove it.

## Claws
If part broken and loose, grip the lower part firmly and tug it off sharply. If the claw bleeds, or if it has already broken off and is

bleeding, apply a firm dressing until the bleeding stops. If the quick is exposed, or the claw is painful, the paw will need to be covered to protect it. May need antibiotic treatment. If broken but firm, dress to relieve discomfort. Seek veterinary treatment – may require anaesthetic to remove claw.

## Collapse

May be due to heart failure, respiratory failure, internal bleeding, shock, diabetes etc.

- Lie dog on its side with neck stretched out. Pull tongue forward and out of mouth to clear air passage. Ensure nothing obstructing airway. Check dog is breathing, heart is beating (feel between ribs behind elbow, easiest on left side), and colour of mucous membranes (gums easiest). Contact vet with this information, and arrange urgent attention.
- If heart is not beating, attempt cardiac massage by squeezing rib cage over lower half of chest and midway between elbow and last rib. Squeeze one to two times per second (use the higher rate for small dogs). Compress chest in a coughlike manner.
- If the dog is not breathing, attempt to ventilate by ensuring the airway is clear, the tongue pulled forward, and pressing over a large area of the ribcage. Press down slowly and firmly, then release. Repeat every two seconds.

## Cuts and grazes

*Small cuts:* Trim away fur with curved scissors, clean with disinfectant/ saline and dress if bleeding. Apply antiseptic cream 3 times daily and keep clean.

*Large cuts* (>1"): Will probably require stitches. Clean, dress if bleeding and contact vet.

*Cut tongue:* These cuts usually bleed profusely, and blood mixed with saliva spreads dramatically. If the dog is kept quiet and not fed or watered the bleeding will usually stop, even if the cut is severe. Most are best checked by a vet, as examination of the mouth is difficult.

*Tips of ears:* Often bleed profusely. Bleeding will stop if you can immobilise the ears. Try using the leg of a pair of tights as a 'head sock'.

## Diarrhoea

Starve for 24 hours. Give a sugar/salt solution (1 pint boiled water, 1 tablespoon sugar, 1 teaspoon salt – or use an electrolyte solution from your vet). Then feed small amounts of chicken/fish/scrambled egg mixed with boiled white rice. If there is blood in the diarrhoea, or it persists after starvation or the dog is unwell, contact the vet.

## Drowning

Pull clear of water, and lay dog on its side, preferably with the head down. If unconscious lift the dog by its back legs to allow water to leave chest. Check breathing. If not breathing, attempt artificial respiration as in 'Collapse' above. Seek immediate veterinary attention.

## Eczema

'Hot spots' (red, moist, exuding pus/serum) especially common over base of tail, or on the cheeks. Often in the summer. Clip away fur, bathe with disinfectant/saline 2–3 times daily, apply antiseptic, stop the dog scratching/biting the spot. Normally require veterinary treatment to treat the underlying cause and the infection.

## Electrocution

Turn off power, or remove dog from power source using a stick, wooden chair etc. **Do not touch** until clear of power source, and then only lightly with the back of the hand in case residual current is present. Check heart and breathing and attempt resuscitation if necessary (see 'Collapse' above). Seek immediate veterinary attention.

## Eyes

*Foreign bodies:* Grass seeds, twigs etc. Removal should only be attempted if the object is protruding from the eye. All cases should be checked by a vet as soon as possible to detect remaining fragments or damage to the cornea.

## Fits

If possible, move dog away from any furniture or objects on which it might injure itself. Do not try to hold or comfort the dog while having a fit – it is likely to bite you. When the fit is over watch out for unpredictable or aggressive behaviour. Most fits are over within minutes. If one persists, or a dog is having repeated fits at short intervals, seek veterinary attention. If the dog recovers from a fit normally, then take it for a check up as soon as is convenient. It may be helpful to take a urine sample, and not to feed the dog for several hours before your appointment in case the vet would like to take a blood sample.

## Fractures

Carry dog back to house or car if possible. Fractures of lower limbs may be splinted, either with a dressing of several layers of cotton wool, or with cardboard cut to length and applied to the limb. Contact the vet immediately.

## Gastric torsion

**Urgent**. Twisted stomach. Especially deep chested breeds (Great Dane, Dobermann, German Shepherd). Usually follows a meal. Dog may belch or attempt to vomit repeatedly. Abdomen swollen behind rib cage. May be very lethargic or collapse. Contact vet immediately you suspect this condition. Avoid the problem by splitting food into two meals. Avoid too much cereal. Don't exercise for some hours following a meal.

## Grass seed

Summer months. Any breed, but especially Spaniels/long haired breeds. Sudden onset of intense irritation of one ear or the other. Shaking of head, scratching. Must be seen by vet as soon as possible.

## Heat stroke

May occur in cars in sunny weather, or at exercise on a hot day. Especially short nosed breeds, obese or dark coloured dogs. Fever, lethargy and collapse may result. Cool down as soon as possible. Place in a cold bath or run a cold hose over dog. Contact vet urgently. May be fatal.

## Injuries

*Stick injury:* Common if sticks are thrown. The stick penetrates the back of the mouth. Should always be checked by a vet. Will usually require general anaesthetic to thoroughly explore the wound for fragments. Commonly cause abscesses in the throat even years after the incident.

## Painkillers

No painkillers should be administered to a dog without first seeking veterinary advice.

Do not use drugs such as paracetamol in case of toxicity, unless specifically advised to do so by your vet.

## Poisoning

Keep the container, or a sample of the poison/plant/baited food. Contact vet immediately. If poison taken recently and vet advises inducing vomiting (not suitable for all poisons) use concentrated salt water or washing soda crystals on the back of the tongue. Keep a sample of the vomit. If the vet advises, milk or fuller's earth (eg in some cat litters) may help to protect the bowel and reduce absorption of toxin.

## Road traffic accident

Take care not to be bitten, even if the dog involved is your own. Apply a muzzle if necessary. If collapsed, move gently to the side of the road, or lift onto a blanket and then move off the road, then treat as for 'Collapse' above. Stop any bleeding. Keep warm. Always aim to take the dog to a vet immediately, even if there are no obvious injuries. If a vet is called out, he will most likely remove the dog to the surgery, so valuable time will have been wasted.

## Stings

Not usually dangerous for mature dogs. If the bee sting is visible, remove it with tweezers. Apply meat tenderiser or a suitable cream (Anthisan). Swelling at the site of the sting is common. An ice pack (eg frozen peas) will help reduce this. If swelling of the mouth/ throat, or more general swelling occurs, if your dog is in great pain, or if it has a severe reaction (weakness/collapse), contact the vet.

## Teeth

*Loose tooth:* Old dogs, particularly breeds like Yorkshire Terriers, often have bad teeth, and when gum and socket erosion is severe some teeth may become loose. The movement of the tooth may annoy the dog. If the tooth is hanging out you may be able to grasp it and pull it out. Otherwise a vet will need to attend to it. Get the dental disease treated as well!

*Fractured tooth:* Caused by chewing stones or bones. Even though a dog may show no pain, this is a painful injury. Should be seen by a vet.

## Ticks

If not annoying the dog – leave. If you consider that it needs to be removed, get a vet to do it.

## Vomiting

Starve for 24 hours. Just give boiled water in small quantities (1 teaspoon to 1 tablespoon/hour initially. Stop if this is brought back up). If vomiting stops, try small amount of chicken/fish/scrambled egg. If the dog appears unwell, there is blood in the vomit or it fails to stop after starvation, contact the vet.

# First aid equipment

Useful items to have in a first aid kit include:

- Soft strong bandage/tape for a muzzle
- Crepe knit bandage
- Adhesive bandage
- Curved, blunt ended scissors
- Cotton wool
- Lint pads
- Tweezers
- Nuggets of washing soda (to use as an emetic)
- Antiseptic cream (eg Savlon)

It is also useful to keep a blanket in the car, for use as a stretcher or for warming an injured dog.

Additional items which may be useful:

- Disinfectant (TCP is a good choice)
- Meat tenderiser or Anthisan for insect stings
- Ice pack or poultice (available from your vet, or a packet of frozen peas can be used)
- Kaolin suspension for diarrhoea

To muzzle a dog, take a length of tape, stand behind the dog and holding the material with both hands. Drape the tape over the top of the muzzle, in front of the eyes, cross it under the chin, and bring the ends back behind the ears. Pull firmly to tighten and tie.

**Remember – always contact your vet if your dog is injured or ill, even if only to receive advice by telephone.**

# CHAPTER 11
# The loss of your dog

Sadly, old age is the final chapter in a dog's life before death. With good care, treatment if needed and luck he will have a long and happy old age, but you must prepare yourself for the day when you will lose him. This is not to say that you should constantly worry about it, but rather to accept that he cannot live forever, and so not be too shocked when the end finally comes.

A survey of British pet owners (Laura and Martyn Lee, *Absent Friend*, Henston) found that 50 per cent of dogs died when between the ages of 10 and 15, and a further 20 per cent when they were over 15 years old. Improved nutrition and veterinary care are increasing the dog's life expectancy all the time. Most of us wish that our dog will die peacefully in her bed, or perhaps suddenly while exercising in a favourite place. This wish partly represents our desire for our dog to die without distress, and partly our wish to be spared the responsibility of requesting euthanasia. Sadly the majority of us will have to make the decision to have our dogs put down. About 75 per cent of pet dogs will be euthanased.

## Euthanasia

The reasons for requesting euthanasia are varied and include advanced old age or chronic incurable disease, behavioural problems, senility, loss of toilet training or incontinence, inability to afford treatment or special care, owners emigrating or moving house. Sometimes it can be a correct decision to put a dog down, but equally right to continue trying to treat it. If you have a firm preference, then let the vet know, otherwise he may continue trying to treat an elderly dog even though you have come to the decision that enough is enough.

Many owners feel guilty when the time comes to request euthanasia. They don't like the thought that they are the ones to decide that their dog's life must end. This is natural and understandable, but we should be aware that euthanasia, performed at the right time, is one of the kindest gifts we can give our dog. The decision as to whether to be with your pet or not is entirely yours. Most people welcome the opportunity to stroke and comfort their dog as euthanasia is carried out, so that they lose consciousness with familiar sounds and smells around. If you are very upset, however, your dog will sense this, and it may unsettle him. Because dogs have no knowledge of what is going to happen, they approach euthanasia without fear, but if you transmit your emotions to him he will know something is wrong.

Do not feel guilty if you cannot face being with your dog. Everyone understands, and no-one expects you to behave in one way or another. If you don't want to be with your dog while euthanasia is performed, but would like to see him afterwards, that is fine.

If your dog is undergoing major surgery, to investigate a tumour for example, it is possible that the operating vet will find that the problem is inoperable, or that completing the surgery will not prolong the dog's life. In such a case you may be asked whether your dog can be euthanased while under the anaesthetic. Hopefully you will have had some warning that this is a possibility, and have been able to discuss it with the vet beforehand. Sometimes this news is unexpected, and an unpleasant surprise. Your vet will only ask this of you if she is sure that it is the best course of action. Because the dog would be asleep anyway, it is the kindest way for euthanasia to be performed. You may not wish to let your dog go without a chance to say good-bye, and the vet will respect this, but please consider whether it is fair to allow the dog to come round from the anaesthetic only to be euthanased soon afterwards.

## What happens?

Euthanasia is almost always performed by the injection of a concentrated solution of barbiturate anaesthetic into a vein in a fore leg. The dog will lose consciousness almost instantly, then stop breathing and finally the heart will stop. This whole process may take a few seconds, or the heart may continue beating for a few minutes.

After euthanasia, muscles and limbs may tremble, and the dog may gasp a few times. These are merely reflex actions, and not signs of life, but can be upsetting to see. Unfortunately, if they occur, they are unavoidable. If you are aware that they might happen, hopefully they will not distress you. Dogs' eyes remain open after death, which can also worry owners experiencing the loss of a pet for the first time. It is also normal for the bowel and bladder to empty themselves once a dog has died.

The vet will check that the heart has stopped, and then if you wish he may leave you alone to say good-bye. Don't feel at all embarrassed to show your emotions. It would be far more surprising if you were not upset, and all staff at the surgery understand your feelings very well.

## Where should it be done?

Most dogs are euthanased at the surgery. From the vet's point of view, the procedure can be carried out most easily there, with skilled help available. This is an advantage for your dog, as there is less chance of any complication occurring, if he were to struggle for instance.

If you are able to plan when you want euthanasia performed, ask the surgery if you can come at a time when no other clients are about, so that the vet can devote more time to you, and you do not have to wait, or be embarrassed because other people are about. If euthanasia is unexpected, because your dog has taken a sudden turn for the worse, explain to the receptionist that you think it will be necessary. She will tell the vet, and hopefully he will be able to see you as quickly as possible, to minimise your upset.

Many owners would like their dogs put to sleep at home. Sometimes people are not aware that this is an option, and sometimes the vet may be reluctant, for whatever reason. Most vets are prepared to perform euthanasia at home, but it is helpful if you are able to give enough notice so that a specific time can be arranged. If your dog deteriorates rapidly and you would like him seen quickly, it is always faster to take him to the surgery.

If your dog is weak, euthanasia at home can be a very peaceful process, with very little disturbance to your dog. If he is still strong, he may struggle more because he is in his home environment. Be sure that the vet knows if he is likely to need to bring help. When you 'phone to arrange the visit, tell the surgery if you wish the vet to take the body away with him. For health, safety and cleanliness reasons the vet will probably have to place the body in a secure container to transport it back to the surgery. This is usually a strong plastic sack, designed for the purpose. Seeing this can be upsetting to some owners, but because many dogs release their bowels and bladder after euthanasia, it is necessary.

The final resting place of our dog is something that concerns most owners greatly. Anxieties are raised by scare stories in the press, and our own imaginations. It is important, amidst the distress of losing a dog, that we shouldn't have to worry that its body will be dealt with unsympathetically.

Most dogs that are euthanased at a veterinary surgery will be cremated. Often if they are put to sleep at home, they will be returned to the surgery for cremation. Dogs may be cremated individually and the ashes returned, or communally. If they are cremated communally, the ashes are usually buried at the pet crematorium. Individual cremation is significantly more expensive, but many owners feel happier with this, and many wish to have their dog's ashes back, whether to keep, scatter or bury. If you are worried about what will happen to your dog's body, ask your veterinary practice what their arrangements are.

# Coping with the loss

The loss of a pet dog is a very traumatic experience. Having had your dog for maybe 12 or 14 years, she is truly a part of the family. You may have had her for years before you had children. You will have many memories, not just of her, but of things associated with her. You may have had her on a special occasion, or she may have belonged to a relative. You must expect to be upset when she is finally gone, however much you had been expecting it, and however well you had steeled yourself.

It is impossible in this text to discuss fully the emotions and thoughts that arise at a time like this and readers should refer to *Absent Friend* by Laura and Martyn Lee (Henston Ltd) which does this excellently.

# Summary

- You will usually have some warning that your dog is nearing the end of his life, and have time to prepare yourself

- Most owners will have to make the decision to choose euthanasia for their dog

- Euthanasia at the right time is usually a kindness, and one of the most important decisions that you will have to make for your dog – don't shrink from that decision

- Decide early on, when you are not in a distressed state of mind, where you would like your dog put to sleep, and how you would like his body disposed of – you may later regret hasty decisions made when he is very ill and you are upset

- When your dog dies, you may have to cope with feelings of guilt, anger and grief

- A new dog can be a great help in dealing with the pain of loss, but you should not be rushed into replacing your old dog

- The death of our pet is the one problem that all owners of elderly dogs are going to have to come to terms with. Everyone is bound to feel grief and anguish when it happens, but if with your help, love and care, your dog has had a happy life and lived its allotted span, then you will have the comfort of knowing that your dog leaves you after a life that has given him as much enjoyment as yourself.

# APPENDIX 1
# Health check list

| How is your dog's ... | What to look for | Disorders |
|---|---|---|
| Thirst | Increase | Kidney failure<br>Liver failure<br>Diabetes mellitus/insipidus<br>Tumours<br>Pyometra<br>Psychological thirst senility/boredom |
| Appetite | Increase | Diabetes mellitus<br>Malabsorbtion from the bowel<br>Boredom |
| | Decrease | Dental disease<br>Kidney failure<br>Liver failure<br>Tumours<br>Painful conditions (eg arthritis)<br>Many diseases |
| | Appetite for strange items | Liver disease<br>Nutritional deficiency<br>Senility |
| Weight | Increasing | Overfeeding<br>Hypothyroidism<br>Cushing's syndrome<br>May be :<br>i) abdominal fluid – heart or liver disease<br>ii) increased liver size<br>iii) abdominal tumour |
| | Decreasing | Poor appetite due to chronic disease, inc. dental disease<br>Wasting diseases – heart, liver, kidney, bowel disorders<br>Tumours |

## The Ageing Dog

| | | |
|---|---|---|
| Breath | Halitosis | Dental disease<br>Kidney failure |
| | Smells of urine | Kidney failure |
| | Smells of acetone | Diabetes mellitus |
| Exercise | Stiff/lame | Arthritis<br>Back/neck pain |
| | Reduced stamina | Heart disease<br>Respiratory disease<br>Arthritis<br>Debilitating diseases |
| Eyesight | Bumping into things, lacking confidence, won't follow titbit held before eyes | Cataracts<br>Retinal disease<br>Brain lesions |
| Hearing | Fails to respond to calling, sleeps deeply, easily startled | Senile deafness<br>Ear infection |
| Breathing | Cough | Heart disease<br>Bronchitis<br>Lung tumours |
| | Rapid/laboured breathing | Heart disease<br>Pneumonia |
| | Frequent sneezing | Foreign body in nose<br>Nasal infection<br>Nasal tumour |
| Urination | Increased frequency | Cystitis (esp. bitches)<br>Prostatic disease (dogs)<br>Kidney failure<br>Diabetes mellitus/insipidus |
| | Increased quantity | Kidney failure<br>Diabetes mellitus/insipidus<br>Pyometra |
| | Straining to pass urine | Cystitis<br>Prostatic disease<br>Bladder stones<br>Tumours of urinary system |
| | Failing to pass urine | Bladder stones<br>Tumours |

|  |  |  |
|---|---|---|
|  | Blood in urine | Cystitis<br>Prostatic disease<br>Tumours |
|  | Incontinence | Increased load (kidney failure, diabetes)<br>Cystitis, prostatic disease, tumours<br>Hormonal incontinence (esp. spayed bitches) |
| Defecation | Appears to strain when passing stools | Constipation<br>Colitis<br>Anal gland impaction<br>Rectal tumour |
|  | Increased frequency | Colitis<br>Poor digestion |
|  | Loose stools | Poor digestion<br>Dietary intolerance<br>Colitis<br>Diarrhoea<br>Liver disease |
|  | Blood in stools | Colitis<br>Severe enteritis<br>Bowel tumour |
|  | Mucus/slime on stools | Colitis |
|  | Pale colour | Liver disease |
|  | Increased quantity | Poor digestion<br>Liver disease |
|  | Absence of stools | Obstruction (foreign body, torsion, tumour) |
| Vomiting | Occasional (once weekly) | May be normal |
|  | Often (daily) | Ulcers<br>Kidney failure<br>Liver disease<br>Stomach tumour<br>Pyometra |
|  | Several times daily | Gastritis/gastro-enteritis<br>Foreign body<br>Bowel obstruction<br>Acute kidney failure<br>Liver disease |

**The Ageing Dog**

| Mental state | Aggressive | Senility<br>Painful conditions (eg arthritis)<br>Brain tumour |
| | Lethargic | Senility<br>Painful conditions<br>Conditions causing lack of energy (heart, respiratory, liver)<br>Boredom |

# Physical examination

| Eyes | Cataracts, cloudy lenses, ulcers, cloudy cornea, conjunctivitis, discharge, warts on eyelids.<br>Difference in sizes of pupils.<br>Swelling around the eyes. |
| Ears | Smell, discharge, excess wax, redness, swelling.<br>Swelling of ear flap (haematoma). |
| Mouth | Smell, tooth scale, red gums (gingivitis), loose teeth, cracked teeth, discoloured teeth, discharge from gums.<br>Growths on gums, lips, lining of mouth.<br>Smell from lip folds. |
| Coat | Thinning, smell, greasy, dry, bald areas.<br>Parasites. |
| Skin | Colour (red, dark etc), scurf, sores, thickening, thinning, calluses.<br>Lumps, swellings (record position and size to monitor change), warts. |
| Paws | Redness, infection, cysts between toes, tumours.<br>Claws - cracked, long, worn on dorsal surfaces |
| Genital organs | *Dog* - discharge from penis/prepuce, tumours, change/difference in size of testicles.<br>*Bitch* - discharge from vulva, mammary tumours. |
| Anal region | Tumours, discharge from anal glands, bleeding from anus.<br>Perineal hernia |

# APPENDIX 2
# Grooming

| | Tasks | Frequency (up to..) |
|---|---|---|
| Eyes | Clean away discharges. Bathe with eye cleaner/cooled boiled water if sticky | Daily |
| | Trim long hairs which lie on eyeballs (Pekes, Shih Tzus etc.) | Fortnightly |
| Ears | Clean any wax or discharge from ear opening | Daily |
| | Use an ear cleaner inside the ear canal – don't put cotton buds etc inside the canal to clean it, just use a pad of cotton wool to wipe away the wax which is brought up by the cleaner | Weekly (or more often) |
| | Pluck hairs from inside the canal (especially Poodles) | Weekly (don't pull all at once) |
| Mouth | Dental care (see Chapter 7) | Daily |
| | Clean out lip folds with saline solution (1 teaspoon salt/1 pint water) if smelly | Daily |
| | Trim long hairs around mouth to keep cleaner | Monthly |
| Coat | Brush and comb coat. A wire 'slicker' brush is useful to remove dead hair from medium to long coated breeds. Cut out any stubborn knots | Daily |
| Skin | Apply hand cream, or cream from a veterinary surgery for the purpose, to calluses to soften them | Daily |
| Paws | Trim long hair from between toes to reduce dirt collection, and protect from grass seeds in summer | Monthly |
| | Clean out dirt which collects between pads | Daily |
| | Clip claws – you may prefer the vet to do this. Aged dogs need more frequent nail clipping through reduced exercise. If you wish to do it, always take a small piece of claw off rather than a large one, to reduce the risk of catching the quick. Frequent | Monthly |

'nibbling' is better than drastic claw amputation. If you make a claw bleed, apply pressure to the point for 1-2 minutes. Guillotine or encircling clippers are more comfortable for the dog than the pliers type

| | | |
|---|---|---|
| Genital organs | Clip hair which is becoming urine soiled from prepuce and vulva areas | Fortnightly |
| | Clean away discharges from prepuce/vulva and seek veterinary advice if present | Daily |
| | If bitch is incontinent, apply Vaseline to area around vulva and inner thighs to prevent urine scalding | Twice daily |
| Anal region | Clip fur away from anus to prevent soiling | Monthly |
| | Express anal glands if you feel capable and your vet has demonstrated the technique | Monthly (or more often) |

# APPENDIX 3
# Checklist for travelling by car

1. Safety and comfort    It is safest for you and your dog if he is kept in the back of a hatchback or estate car, with a strong dog guard fitted. He will be even more secure in a cage or crate. If he is loose in the car, he may be distracting to you, and in case of an accident he will be a danger to himself, your passengers and you through being hurled forwards. If he does travel in the cabin, dog harnesses which attach to the rear seat belts are a good idea. A cosy, familiar bed will help to settle him.

2. Arthritis    If your dog suffers from arthritis or a bad back, it will be uncomfortable or impossible for him to get up and down into the car. If he is small enough, you may lift him in and out. Discourage him from jumping out, as an aged dog may injure himself in doing so. If your dog is large, provide a step of some sort to help him up and down, and reduce the lifting you have to do. Frequent stops to allow him to stretch his legs will reduce the stiffness he suffers from the long period of immobility.

3. Travel sickness    Tablets to help control travel sickness are available from veterinary surgeries. Reduce the problem by withholding food for a few hours before travel.

4. Sedatives    If your dog does become upset when travelling, drugs are available to sedate him. These are not suitable for all elderly dogs, and your veterinary surgeon will advise you. Some sedatives also protect against travel sickness.

5. Toilet stops    Remember that your elderly dog may not be able to go very long before needing to urinate or defecate. Make frequent stops to allow stretching of legs and emptying of bowel and bladder. If incontinence is a problem, remember to have her in a plastic bed or have a boot liner.

6. Water    Many elderly dogs have an increased water need. It is important to allow him all the water he needs. Take a supply in the car.

7.  Heat            All dogs are at risk from heat-stroke or heat stress
                    when travelling in cars, and elderly dogs much
                    more so. Remember that you will be travelling in
                    the front with ventilation cooling you, and you
                    may be unaware of the conditions in the back.
                    With poor ventilation and the lack of shade in a
                    hatchback, overheating is a common and serious
                    problem for dogs in cars, even when moving.

# Checklist for your holiday destination

1.  Will your dog be      Old dogs, although rightly much loved by
    welcome?              ourselves, may not always be welcome guests.
                          Incontinence, odours and barking are some of the
                          reasons your friends or landlady may not be
                          delighted to see your dog accompanying you.

2.  Is your destination   If your dog's mobility is poor, cottages with steep
    suitable?             stairs and slippery floors may pose problems. A
                          holiday where you and the family will be out all
                          day on long hikes which the dog can't cope with
                          will mean him being left for extended periods.
                          Remember that many beaches don't allow dogs
                          on them in the summer, and your dog shouldn't
                          be left in the car. Some holiday cottages which
                          allow dogs stipulate that they shouldn't be left in
                          them unattended.

3.  Remember any          Don't leave medication and special diets behind.
    treatment your        Ensure that you will be able to obtain and cook
    dog is on             any diet which your dog is on.

4.  Note the location     Make sure that you will be able to obtain prompt
    and telephone         attention if needed. Take notes on your dog's
    number of the         medical history with you to help any vet that you
    local veterinary      may need to see when on holiday. Take your
    surgery               vaccination records with you as well.

# APPENDIX 4
# Summary of general care for some common ailments of old age

### Urinary incontinence/reduced bladder control

i)     Consult your vet to get treatment if possible (eg cystitis, hormonal incontinence, diabetes)
ii)    Allow frequent opportunity for urination
iii)   DON'T RESTRICT WATER unless approved by your vet
iv)    Use suitable bedding material (eg veterinary bedding) to keep your dog dry when she leaks
v)     Move her sleeping area to a place with a waterproof floor (eg kitchen)
vi)    Apply Vaseline around vulva and groin to protect from urine scald, and bathe soiled areas as necessary
vii)   Don't punish your dog, as anxiety will only worsen the problem
viii)  Other disorders may aggravate the condition (eg arthritis may make a dog unwilling or unable to go outside) and may need treatment
ix)    Enzyme odour eliminators and stain removers are useful in cleaning up accidents

### Faecal incontinence

i)     Consult your vet to get treatment if possible (eg diarrhoea, colitis)
ii)    Allow frequent opportunity for defecation
iii)   Change diet – change feeding times; add fibre if stools are too soft; use a highly digestible, low bulk food (eg extruded pellet food) if excess quantity is the problem
iv)    Move her sleeping area to an area with an easily cleaned floor
v)     Clean soiled skin and fur frequently
vi)    Reassure her that you are not angry with her, as incontinence is distressing for elderly dogs, and colitis in particular is aggravated by stress
vii)   Remember that other disorders, such as arthritis, may be responsible, and treat them if possible
viii)  Enzyme odour eliminators and stain removers are helpful for cleaning up accidents

## The Ageing Dog

### Arthritis
i)    If treatment is available and effective, use it – arthritis is painful
ii)   Provide comfortable, warm bedding; consider using a heated pad in the bed
iii)  Reduce to a minimum the steps and slippery floors that your dog has to cope with
iv)  Massage of affected limbs and joints often help relieve stiffness
v)   Exercise is beneficial, but should be tailored to your dog's ability; several gentle walks a day improve joint mobility; a long strenuous walk will bring increased stiffness the next day

### Blindness/poor eyesight
i)    Keep changes of furniture position in your house, and of garden furniture, to a minimum
ii)   Avoid the need for him to climb steps and negotiate obstacles
iii)  Exercise in familiar places where your dog can remember the route
iv)  Talk to him frequently both at exercise and in the home, to reassure him and help him orientate himself
v)   Keep him on the lead when near roads or other potential hazards, like water
vi)  Fence off ponds or pools in the garden
vii) Warn strangers and children of his disability so that they don't startle or frighten him

### Deafness
i)    Ensure that there isn't a treatable reason for his deafness, such as ear infections or wax build up.
ii)   Avoid startling him, especially when at sleep or rest
iii)  Keep him on the lead when near roads for his safety
iv)  Try to keep within his line of sight at exercise, and don't let him wander out of your sight either

# Index

## K

Kennel cough 77
Kennels 76
Kidneys 18

## L

Leaving the aged dog 59
Lethargy 37
Lice 79
Life expectancies 3
Liver 17

## M

Mammary glands
 lumps 20
Mange mites 80
Medication 106
Minerals 86
Mouth
 diseases 25
 stick injuries 113
Mucus 14, 16
Muscles and joints 4
Musculoskeletal
 system 7

## N

Neutering 80
NSAIDs (Non-steroidal
 anti-
 inflammatories) 10
Nuclear sclerosis 29
Nutrition 83

## O

Obesity 41, 64, 93, 105
 and heart disease 12
 in bladder control 19
 overheating 42
Oedema 13
Osteochondrosis 9

## P

Painkillers 113
Parasites
 external 78
 internal 78
Perianal adenoma 22, 81
Plaque 26
Poisoning 113
Polyps 16
PRA (Progressive retinal
 atrophy) 30
Prostate gland 21
Proteins 83
Pyometra 20

## R

Radiotherapy 36
Reproductive system 19
Respiratory system 14
Retinal diseases 30
Road traffic accident 114
Roughage 87
Roundworms 78

## S

Scratching
 ear 32
Senility 39, 58
Sertoli cell tumour 34
Sight 4
Skin 32
Sleep 37
Slippery floors 54
Soft palate 14
Spaying 21
Spine 9
Spondylosis 9
Stairs 53
Stings 114
Stress 75
Swimming 67
Swimming pools 54
Synovial fluid 8

## T

Tapeworms 78
Tartar 25, 27, 73
Tears 30
Teeth
 first aid 114
Temper 38
Testosterone 24
Thirst 17
Thyroid gland 23
Thyroxin 23
Ticks 79
 first aid 114
Toothpaste 74
Travelling 76
Tumours 34
 benign 34
 malignant 34
 mammary glands 20
 prostrate 81
 testicular 22, 81
 treatment 101

## U

Ulcers 16
 of the eyes 30
Ultrasound 100
Urea 18
Urinary system 18
Urine analysis 99

## V

Vaccinations 77
Vertebrae 9
Vitamins 87, 88
Vomiting 16, 17, 18, 114

## W

Walks 66, 67, 68
Warts 33
 on eyelids 30
Water 87
Womb infections 20
Worming 78

## X

X-rays 100

## Y

Young children 60
Younger dogs 59

## Record of illness and medication*

| Date | Signs shown/ diagnosis | Medication given/ surgical procedure | Coments |
|---|---|---|---|
|  |  |  |  |

Ask your veterinary surgeon to write down the name of the injections or tablets prescribed.

* To include medication given for treatment and prevention of disease, ie antibiotic injections, chemical control of heat, worm doses etc.

# Other publications available from Henston

All titles are available from high street bookshops,
veterinary practices and large pet stores.

## DOGLOPAEDIA

The new edition of this best-selling and comprehensive guide is relevant to all
owners. It has been extensively revised and reorganised. Quick and easy
reference is now possible on all topics for owning and enjoying a dog.
Doglopaedia is *the* essential reference book for all caring dog owners. **£8.95**

## CATLOPAEDIA

All caring cat owners will find the information and guidance given invaluable
for gaining a more thorough understanding of their cat. This understanding
will enable a happier and more fulfilling relationship between cat and owner.
The information given includes choosing a kitten, feeding, first aid and
nursing and coping with common cat problems. Cat lovers will find the
Catlopaedia indispensable. **£8.95**

## BOOK OF THE BITCH

Written by experts, this book is relevant for all those who are considering
owning a bitch. The more you know about your bitch the happier and
healthier she is likely to be. This book contains vital information and advice on
recognising sickness and what action should be taken. Every caring bitch
owner will value and treasure this comprehensive guide. **£9.95**

## ABSENT FRIEND

This book is for anyone who loves, lives with or works with animals. Pet
owners can use the book as a guide to coping with problems associated with
pet loss. The authors have experience in the veterinary field and in
bereavement counselling, enabling them to fully examine both practical and
emotional issues. **£4.95**

## HOW TO BUY A HORSE

Buying a horse or pony should be a great thrill and the start of a long and
happy relationship. A bad buy however, not only implies a financial loss, but
also a potentially arduous and frustrating experience for both horse and
owner. Pit-falls are highlighted and helpful hints abound to ensure that would
be horse owners are never "taken for a ride". **£4.95**